Rose,

To your cont [barcode] being a landlord. This book is to help you. Please call me with your questions.

Russ

P.S. Thank You for trusting us with ALL your insurance protection.

Growing Your Real Estate Empire

Secrets from a 30-Year Insider

By Russ Castle

Table of Contents

Dedication V

Disclaimer vii

Foreword by Mike Stromsoe ix

Introduction – Who is Russ Castle, author of "Growing Your Real Estate Empire"? xv

Part 1: Before You Invest a Dime

Chapter 1 So You Want to be a Real Estate Investor? 3

Chapter 2 What it takes to be a successful landlord? 7

Part 2: Professionals Never Wing It And "Wingers" Lose Money!

Chapter 3 Why Do Most Landlords Prefer "Residential"? 13

Chapter 4 Tenant Occupancy – Residential or Mixed-Use buildings? 19

Chapter 5 The Buy and Hold Versus Flip Conundrum 23

Chapter 6 To Self-Manage or Property Manage 29

Part 3: It's A Business – Manage It Well and Reap the Rewards

Chapter 7 Expert Tips on First Impression 37

Chapter 8 Pets & Your Tenants 43

Chapter 9 Why Courts Like Tenants More Than Landlords 47

Chapter 10 11 Insider Secrets to Saving on Your Rental and More 53

Chapter 11 Tenants are Not Your Friends 57

Chapter 12 Rental Agreements Musts 61

Chapter 13 Landlord Do's & Don'ts with Tenants 65

Chapter 14 What Type of Tenant Do You Want 69

Chapter 15 Are Section 8 Tenants Right for You? 75

Chapter 16 Best Time of the Year to Get a Tenant 79

Chapter 17 Handling Evictions the Right Way 83

Chapter 18 Quick Action for Vacancies - Marketing Your Properties 89

**Part 4: Protect Your Property
– And ALL Your Assets – From Financial Disaster**

Chapter 19 What to Look for in an Insurance Agent & How to Find a Good One 95

Chapter 20 Why Insurance Specialists are Worth Their Weight in Gold..... 101

Chapter 21 Having the Right Insurance Protection – What You Need to Know to Succeed 105

Chapter 22 Smart Investors Build an Expert Team.. 113

Chapter 23 Secrets to Saving Money on Your Real Estate Premiums 117

Chapter 24 Landlord Insurance – Why is it needed................................. 121

Chapter 25 Ins & Outs of Umbrella Liability Insurance 125

Chapter 26 The Inside Scoop on Admitted & Non-Admitted Insurance Companies 129

Chapter 27 What is a BOP or CPP and Why You Need to Know................. 133

Chapter 28 How "Blanketing" Can Keep You Out of Trouble........................ 137

Chapter 29 Vacant vs Occupied & Your Liability.. 141

Chapter 30 Tips for Insuring Multiple Locations.. 145

Chapter 31 The Insurance Claims Process & What You Need to Know.... 149

Chapter 32 One Size Does Not Fit All.. 153

Part 5: Maximize Your Financial Windfall

Chapter 33 Tax Benefits of Rental Properties 159

Chapter 34 1031 Exchange & Capital Gains.. 163

Chapter 35 Real Estate Investing & Inheritance... 167

Chapter 36 Insider Investment Tips... 173

Conclusion 177

Dedication

This book is dedicated to my father, Jack Castle. Without him I would not be where I am today, both personally and professionally. He was my first mentor. He provided an opportunity for me to join the "office." Thanks DAD! My mother, Raegene Castle as well. She worked in the agency when I joined and was instrumental in my becoming an "employee" there.

To my wife, Mary, who is always behind me 100%. To my boys, John & Patrick, who are becoming the men I have always hoped they would be. Without you three, I would not be doing what I do. You are the reason for my life. I Love You.

To my dear friend, Mike Stromsoe (You are not only my friend, you are my mentor and I am one of your biggest fans); without you this book would NOT be possible. Thanks for your insight and vision. My agency would not be where it is without knowing you many years ago.

Finally, to all my family, friends and clients; you make it all worthwhile.

Disclaimer

The Publisher and the Authors make no representations or warranties with respect to the accuracy or completeness of the contents of this work and specifically disclaim all warranties, including without limitations warranties of fitness for a particular purpose. No warranty may be created or extended by sales or promotional materials. The advice and strategies contained herein may not be suitable for every situation.

Neither the Publisher nor the Authors shall be liable for damages arriving here from. The fact that an organization or website is referred to in this work as a citation and/or a potential source of further information does not mean that the authors or publisher endorse the information the organization or website provides or recommendations it may make.

Foreword
Building Empires - Been There And Still Doing It

Written by Mike Stromose, The Unstoppable Profit Producer Author, Speaker, Entrepreneur and Coach

When Russ Castle called to tell me, he was publishing a book to help people Grow Their Real Estate Empire, it was one of those moments when that little "natural buzz" comes to mind. I instantly knew that this book will help thousands of people. Many who think they already know everything they need to know about the real estate game.

Russ Castle is a master at what he does. Russ knows about real estate-protecting it, managing it and buying it. All of the systems. The positioning of the insurance products, the vendors and everything associated with it. Many of these things no one else knows like Russ Castle. My heart hung heavy and my shoulders, too, when Russ called me to ask if I would simply take a look at a few chapters of the new book and perhaps say something about what I saw. Given that Russ is a friend and a master, I gritted my teeth and said simply that I would, knowing in my heart that no matter how much a master of real estate Russ is, there are very very few folks who can turn that skill into a book that people read, and then read again because the words and the way they are arranged capture the imagination of all as all great stories do. I was afraid that when I began to read his book, I would have to tell him the truth: books are hard to do, Russ, but what the heck, you did a good job, and there are so many other things you're good at cama you'll never even remember this after a few years go by and the pain of harsh critics goes away, then you'll discover a brand-new day. That's what I thought I would have to say to Russ once I took a look at what he sent my way. But, Russ, I have to say it: you are now a master of books, too!! And that's what I find myself saying to you, fellow reader. That Russ Castle is not only a master of the subject within the covers of this book, but of something much more profound, something much deeper than the subject of real estate and protecting it. Russ knows how the world of words works. He knows how stories are told. He knows why the world needs great story tellers. Russ teaches you between the covers of this book how to understand real estate like no other. And he does that in the best way of all: he tells a story, his own story and then another, and he tells even another story better than the ones before. Each in his own words from his own life experiences to create the knowledge that will help you better understand how to grow and protect your real estate empire.

It is an honor and a privilege to continue to learn from Russ Castle. I am proud to introduce you to Russ Castle of **"Insurance by Castle"** and the author of this book – **"Growing Your Real Estate Empire**

If you have any questions about Russ Castle, don't hesitate to contact me.

Mike Stromsoe
Murrieta 2017
http://www.siaonline.com
http://www.unstoppableprofitproducer.com

What Real Estate Owners are saying about Russ Castle:

- "Putting all of our properties on one commercial policy reduced our insurance expense by 50 percent, as compared to individual policies for each property through Farmers." - *Julie Carson, Sacramento, CA &Client since 2013*

- "Great response to questions and insurance needs. Staff is always polite makes you feel important. We know that our coverage takes care of all our needs." - *Chris Miller, Cameron Park, CA & client since 1988*

- "Responsive to questions. Saved a lot of money in the process." – *Dennis Royer, Redwood City, CA & Realtor and client since 2016*

- "Russ has been a great help over the years. He has assisted us with our commercial insurance needs. We recommend him highly." - *Martha Lancesremere, Menlo Park, CA & Client since 2006*

- "Coming up on forty years of trouble-free service says it all." – *Harry Gossard, Lincoln, CA & client since 1980*

- "Great service at a great price. Easy to set up and get things going." - *Orlando Gonzalez, Fresno, CA & client since 2014*

- "I have owned rental property for 40 years, I do shop insurance. I find Insurance by Castle to be the best I can find..." - *Virgil Havener, Hemet, CA & client since 2012*

- "Solid reliable service." - *Kim Bergeson, Oxnard, CA & client since 2014*

- "Over the years that we have been with Castle Insurance, we have literally saved THOUSANDS of dollars... Thank you!" *- Greg White, Fresno, CA & client since 2008*
- "We saved considerably by switching. It was easy to accomplish and your office staff were great." *- Roy Meazell, Pacific Grove, CA & client since 2013*
- "I have been a client with Castle Insurance for over 30 years. I have found all the staff to be very helpful." *– Margaret Maguire, Redwood City, CA & client since 1983*
- "Customer service is absolutely the best. From providing certificates, making changes and giving quotes. They are always extremely quick and responsive." *– Larry Aikins, Redwood City, CA & Realtor to landlords and client since 1984*
- "You give me peace of mind that my property is in good hands if something happened there." *- Juan Navarro, Watsonville, CA & client since 2006*
- "Castle Insurance bundled all of my rental properties which saved me $$. During refinancing of several properties, they have changed the mortgagee clause fast and accurately." *- James Bowman, Lakeside, OR & client since 2006*
- "Excellent rate, excellent Agency." *– Nini Sharma, South San Francisco, CA & client since 2014*
- "Your service is great and always take care of our needs very promptly!" *- Derrick Scelzi, Fresno, CA & client since 2003*
- "You saved me money and everything went through without any problems, thanks." *- Mike Garcia, Moorpark, CA & client since 2013*

- "Best rates. Always get prompt response when I have a question or need something." - *Christine Drier, Sacramento, CA & client since 2014*
- "We love Insurance by Castle. Russ and his team are professional and knowledgeable. I highly recommend them for your insurance needs." - *Myah Waldvogel, Vacaville, CA & insurance company representative and client since 2005*
- "Great customer service! All the people at Castle are very friendly and super knowledgeable. And even if they don't know a detail, they will find out and get back to us right away." - *Tony Marques, Los Altos, CA & client since 1985*
- "I am always able to reach someone; my questions are answered and the premium rates are competitive." - *Gary Lindsey, Roseville, CA & client since 2006*
- "I always get excellent service when I call to add another rental property or make changes to my umbrella policy." – *Jerry Collins, Redwood City & client since 1991*
- "Great customer service, friendly staff, and we always get the help we need!" - *Scott Kirksey, Redwood City & client since 2009*
- "Castle helped our family through the transition after the passing of our parents greatly. Always kind and professional and willing to get the absolute best for their clients. Highly recommended for all your insurance needs." - *Evangeline Howard, Bakersfield, CA & client since 2016*

- "We reduced our hazard insurance expense significantly by obtaining one commercial policy. The service is comparable to what I received from other agencies offering much more expensive insurance." - *Julie Lewis, Sacramento, CA & client since 2013*

- "Castle Insurance saved us lots of money on the insurance for our rental houses. My questions get answered in a timely and professional manner by the friendly staff." - *Harold Wright, Desert Hot Springs, CA & client since 2012*

- "I like that Castle Insurance takes care of my insurance and all its aspects requiring very little from me. I tend to be very busy so I appreciate not having to be returning calls or responding to messages when necessary. I also think they are trustworthy and reliable." - *Cynthia Perez, San Jose, CA & client since 2013*

- "Made finding insurance with a good carrier easy and affordable. Always answers questions and concerns promptly." - *Getchel Wilson, Redondo Beach, CA & client since 2008*

Introduction – Who is Russ Castle, author of "Growing Your Real Estate Empire"?

This book is about providing the tips and tricks to owning residential rental property from an owner, investor, and insider's point of view. The author, Russ Castle, is a third-generation independent insurance broker in Silicon Valley, California, and he shares his story and tips to help you succeed. Through his experiences as a rental property owner, a business owner, and an independent insurance broker who specializes in residential rental for California, he comes to the residential rental market with a unique perspective from his various points of view. He gives you the "insider secrets" to saving on expenses including what to look for in properties, tenants, and so much more!

It all started with his grandfather, Ray Kidder, in the 1940's (his mother's father). Ray was an independent insurance agent in San Carlos. Then, in the early 1960's, his father, Jack, got in the industry. All through his childhood he would go into his father's agency and see how Dad did things. Then, in 1992, he joined the "office." His grandfather, his father and Russ have insured landlords since the very beginning.

As he acknowledges, looking back it's always good to see what leads us to where we are today. And like most, family is a big part of his journey. His father, along with a long-time client, pointed out the advantages of having other people pay your mortgage as a big deciding factor. Both of these men acknowledged how to get the rental property to work for you. Primarily, if you get in at the right cost, and do the right things, that investment pays for itself and provides you an income. If you save enough to purchase the property at a competitive price and a good location, you know you can rent it for enough money to cover the basic expenses (mortgage payment, taxes, insurances, etc.). In most cases, if you bought the rental at a good price, the rent payments are more than the sum total of expenses. Moreover, while the property is increasing in value, your equity will be increasing as well. You can then use that equity and/or additional money to continue buying rentals and keep increasing your investments. This process can provide a nice steady income.

Today, Russ is happy to be where he is and delighted to share with you not only his journey, but how you, too, can be successful. Learn from his successes as well as his mistakes, and as you read this book, apply it to your life, and your business.

This book isn't meant to be read in one or two sittings. It's meant to be studied and highlighted. And most importantly, it's meant to help you in this process. The outcome will be your success.

Russ has found that in building your business, it's important to understand your passion. What is important to you? Is it family, friends, time off, travel, money, wealth management, etc.? Are you looking to supplement your income or do you want to go full-time? When you know the goals, you want out of your business, then you are better able to move towards those goals.

It's also important to remember that in real estate investing, timing is critical. Know that real estate fluctuates in value and, often, that is based on current circumstances such as the real estate market, economy, population, growth, availability of properties, etc. As you go through this book, be sure to ask yourself, "Is this the right time for me to invest?

We believe the right time to jump in is now! The opportunities are boundless and the potential is greater than ever before. Plus, armed with the knowledge from this book, you will learn the right way to do things, avoiding those costly mistakes, and setting yourself up for wealth, happiness, and above all else, a business you love. Let's go!

Part 1

Before You Invest a Dime

Chapter 1
So You Want to be a Real Estate Investor?

Before even starting down the road of owning real estate as a landlord—You need to answer the question:

What is your end game?

By starting at the end, you can then get a better understanding of how and why you are purchasing residential rental properties. Knowing this helps with every aspect of the business, from deciding on properties, to working with tenants, and everything in between.

Some people are becoming landlords of one form or another for "additional income." These people might still have a regular job and want that extra income coming in, are retired or soon to be retired and want to continue making income. Others are becoming landlords as a profession and want to make this their career. They are in it for the long haul.

Although all of these options work, but you need to decide what you want for yourself.

Once you have decided on your overall reason, you can then start to work backwards and get a glimpse of how it is going to happen. The goal is truly just to get a good idea what it all looks like prior to getting started. You need to do your homework. You will be more successful if you have a plan. Then you can follow your plan and make adjustments as needed along the way.

The following questions are a small sampling of what you need to answer before starting down the road to becoming a landlord:

- When do I want to start and for how long of a period do I want to do this?
- How much of my time is available for the rental property?
- Am I going to self-manage or hire a property management company to assist in some or all the aspects of the business?
- How am I going to come up with the down payment?
- Do I want to be the sole owner? Do I want to have partners? Do I want to be strictly an investor? Or do I want a combination of these?
- If you want to keep purchasing additional locations, where are the additional down payments for these properties coming from?
- What type of landlord do I want to become? Do I want to work with Single Family Residential – Multi-Unit Residential – Commercial Retail – Commercial Warehouse – Mixed used (both residential and commercial in the same building), etc.?
- What kind of financing is available to purchase and maintain the properties?
- Have I done my homework on the expenses expected (including mortgage payments, insurance, property taxes, etc.) so I have a good understanding of my potential income and expenses moving forward?

- Do I have money for repairs and have I budgeted accordingly? This is especially true if the building needs work done before you can rent it out.
- How much of a cash "safety net" do I have for vacancies or unseen expenses?
- What is the rental market in your area like? Is it a renter's market with low prices or landlord's market with high rents?
- What type of personality do I have? Do I stress out over the little things, or can I pretty much take charge and get it done without losing sleep? Just knowing yourself better here will enable you to plan accordingly. If you happen to stress easily, then pay attention to what you can do to avoid more stress. Even having lists of what needs to be done and procedures in place helps.

While most of these questions seem basic, and there are many more that could go on this short list, you need to go through each one and think it through. This will allow you to plan accordingly and make better decisions.

Once you have a firm grasp on your end game and the answers to your pre-planning questions, you can start to look at what is available for sale. Most people will use a realtor that works in the area where you want to purchase, specialize in the type of real estate you are looking to buy.

In my area of California, you need to be pre-approved for a loan and ready to make the offer sometimes within days of the original listing. More seasoned owners have a network where they can be told of property that is available before it hits the street or maybe it will be a sale WITHOUT ever hitting the street. Either way, you need to be ready to move quickly to secure the location and get it at the best possible price and terms.

If your end game is to be a landlord for many years, you might use the equity in the property at a later date for some expenses you anticipate. For example, I had one client that used some of the equity in his rental property to travel with his family once a year after he retired from his "day job." You need to talk to your financial advisor about some of the advantages and best ways to get your property to work FOR YOU.

I had another client who borrowed from his 401K to get the down payment on his first residential rental. Over the years he fixed up the rental and refinanced it and used that equity to purchase the next residential rental. After just 10 years, and a lot of hard work, he was up to almost 300 rental units. The cash flow for these rentals provided a sizable income. Does that sound like something you'd like to do? It certainly can be achieved with the right knowledge, experience, and hard work.

Now that you know your end game, let's dig into more detail on what it all looks like.

HERE IS WHAT TO DO NEXT:
- **DRAFT YOUR PLAN**
- **CONTACT ME TO DISCUSS YOUR SPECIFIC SITUATION AND GET ANSWERS TO YOUR BURNING QUESTIONS. EMAIL – Russ@InsuranceByCastle.com or PHONE – 800-644-6443 extension 101.**

Chapter 2
What it takes to be a successful landlord?

First of all, what is driving you now to become a landlord? Is the idea of owning property and being a landlord your motivating factor? Or do you desire a source of additional income? Do you have practical business skills or management skills necessary to be successful in this business?

Often times, the idea of owning and renting property can be seen as an easy way to increase wealth and personal assets. However, to be successful, one needs to remember that this is a business venture and needs to be realistically viewed as such. There is so much more to it than just buying property and reaping the rewards. It's important to understand your motivations so you can make more of the right decisions and less of the wrong ones. It will also help you in determining what types of properties interest you most as each type has its own advantages and disadvantages. For example, over the years I've learned owning residential rentals is a better fit for me. It is easier to get tenants in my area for residential units. Plus, the rents cover all the expenses (mortgage, taxes, insurance, and maintenance). And I enjoy this type of work.

For commercial buildings, there are various types of rentals (warehouse vs. retail). Personally, I feel these types of rentals are harder to keep. However, I know many clients who feel the exact opposite. Choose whatever is in your comfort level.

Your personality and your goals also come into play a great deal when deciding which way to go as well. Each type of property ownership offers its own benefits and risks in being successful. You need to decide early on—do you want to focus on residential properties or do commercial office rentals and commercial warehouses excite you most? Or would a combination of both be a great fit for you? Have an understanding of what it takes to own, rent, and maintain these properties. Then move forward with that in mind.

Residential is much different than the various types of commercial buildings. Without a passion for either area, you will not succeed. I have found it best to have a goal of where you want to be in five or ten years from starting. At this time, you can see if your plan can be attained in the timeframe you have set. Set REALISTIC expectations. Sometimes your plan might be more aggressive than what you want or the market in your area can sustain. Review your goals periodically and adjust as needed along your journey.

One thing to remember when investing in real estate is that reputation is critical, which is why it's important to find the right match in tenants, contractors, realtors, etc. Word can quickly spread if you become a landlord that is never pleased, doesn't fix what is needed, or simply doesn't care. Go in knowing that you will work to the best of your ability. You want to do a great job and get the respect of your tenants so not only do they stay longer, but they recommend your properties to others.

Remember, too, the importance of the reputations of those you work with along the way. This is why it is so critical to work with those you trust. Through the years you will find the right team that is an asset to you and you enjoy working with. Having a good "team" will make this journey easier.

The other option, when owning rental property, is to use a property management company like I do for my rentals. I have a full time "day job" and use the property management company to handle the daily tasks. The only item I handle is collecting the rent and paying the mortgage. The choice is up to you—how many or how few of the tasks you want to handle. Our book should help you decide what is best for you.

HERE IS WHAT TO DO NEXT:
- **DO YOUR DUE DIGLIENCE AND DETERMINE WHERE YOU WANT TO FOCUS YOUR ENERGY**
- **DRAFT YOUR EXPERT ADVISOR DESCRIPTION. IN OTHER WORDS, WHO DO YOU WANT AND NEED ON YOUR TEAM OF EXPERTS**
- **CONTACT ME TO DISCUSS YOUR SPECIFIC SITUATION AND GET ANSWERS TO YOUR BURNING QUESTIONS. EMAIL – Russ@InsuranceByCastle.com or PHONE – 800-644-6443 extension 101.**

Part 2

Professionals Never Wing It And "Wingers" Lose Money!

Chapter 3
Why Do Most Landlords Prefer "Residential"?

Know that in real estate investing, a big part of what you do will be dealing with tenants. Residential and commercial tenants differ drastically. Let's break it down.

Residential:

- Residential investing normally consists of homes, duplexes, apartments, etc. These rentals are more for the tenants' personal use as opposed to using them for business.
- Residential rentals – Houses and duplexes usually have longer term tenants who take better care and pride of the rental and therefore, scalability can be better with apartments. Apartments tend to be cheaper, whereas homes tend to be nicer. Multi-family residential rentals (apartments) are often considered the easiest properties to get tenants for a number of reasons. One prime example we are seeing today is retirement downsizing. Traditionally, families make the move to a house in order to spend the child rearing years in a larger space. However, once children have grown up and moved on, there's no longer a need for all those extra bedrooms, as well as the maintenance required for backyards and other amenities that are no longer seeing regular use. Retirement couples often "downsize" to an apartment to enjoy retirement with fewer

housekeeping responsibilities, and more income from the sale of a home. While this is a well understood and documented real estate phenomenon, it's the scale at which it is now happening that is remarkable. Keeping up with the supply to satisfy this growing demand will be extremely lucrative for apartment investors. Something to consider for sure. And this is only one example.

- Multi-unit residential properties are easier to get tenants due to lower rent, which is a real benefit. Having a multi-unit residential building allows you to spread the expense. For example, if you have a ten-unit apartment and one unit is not rented, then you are only looking at missing approximately 10% of the total revenue. However, if you have a single-family home that is not rented, then you are losing out on 100% of that revenue. My experience is that while a single-family home has the potential for 100% of revenue loss, homes get better tenants (if you do it correctly) and stay longer at higher rents. Plus, they usually will take better care of the property. The apartment rental price is usually lower and, thus, you get what you pay for. Conversely, I have seen many commercial rentals go vacant for long periods of time. It is best to rent to the type of tenants that you know will stay. Of note, too, is although commercial rentals might go vacant for long periods of time, most commercial rentals can get long-term leases.

- In some areas, residential apartments are month-to-month. But we are finding that more and more residential rentals are now only being offered for a one-year lease or longer. So, the potential for a vacancy can be more in an apartment, but the rental loss of revenue is less due to it not affecting the entire building.

- Region can also play a factor. It's a fact, rental properties in most of California these days are high and those that rent will pay higher rates. However, the good news is that these tenants often take better care of their property so you will have fewer hassles and expenses down the road. That might not be the case in other regions, so do your homework for your area.

Commercial:

Commercial rentals consist of many types of properties including offices, warehouses, retail centers, buildings, commercial land, etc.

When considering the right option in commercial real estate, consider the following:

- Commercial retail can be advantageous for long-term tenants. These tenants often operate their own businesses in these locations and don't want to go through the hassles of moving and potentially losing customers. Good for you—less time and effort in finding new tenants and rental turnover.
- Commercial warehouses can have the same advantage if it's an established business.

- There is a higher chance of exposure for an insurance claim with commercial rentals especially retail businesses. More traffic in and out of the location vs. residential rentals with individuals or families.
- You need to know the ins and outs of the various types of commercial rentals and to whom and how they should be rented. I have experience with clients involved in:
  1. A commercial retail storefront. This is probably one that is similar to residential. Most of these buildings are small in size and easier to keep a tenant. What retail business wants to move once they have an established location? Not many. These leases can be for longer periods of time.
  2. A commercial warehouse rental. These can be either for a business to operate in or for storage for a business (like a construction company). The pros of these are the upkeep might not be very much. The amenities are few. The downside is that there could be a longer period of time between tenants as these renters are specific for this type of building (and possibly land). But, like the retail spaces, the tenants that are operating these businesses are often longer-term tenants.

HERE IS WHAT TO DO NEXT:

- **DETERMINE IF YOU ARE BEST SUITED FOR RESIDENTIAL OR COMMERCIAL INVESTING**
- **CONTACT ME TO DISCUSS YOUR SPECIFIC SITUATION AND GET ANSWERS TO YOUR BURNING QUESTIONS. EMAIL – <u>Russ@InsuranceByCastle.com</u> or PHONE – 800-644-6443 extension 101.**

Chapter 4
Tenant Occupancy – Residential or Mixed-Use buildings?

As a landlord, you need to decide what type of tenant you want. There are three main types:

- Residential – Rental homes through apartment buildings
- Commercial buildings – Retail, warehouses, manufacturing, etc.
- Mixed use. This is usually a multi-story building with both residential and retail businesses or something similar included. Often times the retail business can be on one floor and the residential units above. This includes both of the above.

When renting residential units, there are two main divisions - single family units and multi-family units (i.e., duplex, triplex, quads and apartments). Typically, rental terms range from monthly to a lease for a few years as we've previously discussed. The single-family rentals usually house families, which can mean longer term tenants as often once a family moves in, they stay. However, if a vacancy occurs, there is a 100% loss of revenue for this rental, whereas if it was a vacancy in an apartment, it would only mean a percentage of the building is lost rent and not a total loss of revenue.

Apartment rentals tend to be more affordable than a single-family unit.

Commercial retail tenants have long term leases as well. Commercial manufacturing and warehouses often rent for longer terms. However, there can be longer vacancies between tenants as it can be more challenging at times to find a business that needs space than say a family that needs a home.

No matter which type you choose, safety and zoning regulations are a priority to understand before purchasing the property. Review the regulations in the area before you invest. Consider everything that can come into play including having all these set up properly: fire alarms, elevators, wiring, handicap access, sprinkler systems, etc.

You will be required to do inspections regularly and these should always be up-to-date. This is not only a requirement, but gives you peace of mind as well.

Here are a few other things to consider in helping you decide what might be a good fit for you, especially when it comes to mixed-use buildings:

- Let's say your business depends on visitors and foot traffic. When you consider choosing a location that is around a residential area whose residents might buy your products or services, that's a win/win. Having your commercial property in these key areas can be good marketing as many of your customers can be those that just happen to stop by your location as they walk past it or see signs in the area. You can see the benefit there!

- Those customers that are in walking distance, are usually a mix of short-term and long-term tenants, which can be a real benefit.
- In many downtown areas in California, mixed-use buildings happen to be the majority of new buildings being built. It helps promote the residential units downtown and requires less driving for these tenants. Another win/win!

When considering owning in a mixed-space environment, take your time and review the area prior to purchasing.

Things to look for include: Do the residents take good care of their property? You don't want your property to be viewed unfavorably because of the neighborhood and that can easily happen. Also, check out the other businesses in the area. How do they look? Would you want to do business with them? Once again, when you do your homework prior to buying, it can save you many headaches down the road.

Another great way to tell is to drive around at different times during the day, including rush hour. See if there are any problems that you might encounter. Look for things such as too much traffic, unsavory people walking the streets, or the area being a ghost town. You might discover that although the area is well developed, no one truly is around in the area, so the advantage of foot traffic is lessened. By driving around, you will find out what you need to know. It's amazing what a difference a few hours can make in your search as well, which is why we recommend the different timing.

The bottom line is this—does the space you are considering meet all your needs? To best determine that, it helps to write down exactly what you want out of your units and then write down the pros and cons of the units you are considering. Armed with this knowledge, you'll be able to make the right decision for you.

HERE IS WHAT TO DO NEXT:

- **DETERMINE IF YOU WANT RESIDENTIAL, COMMERCIAL, MANUFACTURING, MIXED USE, ETC.**
- **START TO FAMILARIZE YOURSELF WITH SAFETY AND ZONING REGULATIONS IN YOUR AREA**
- **CONTACT ME TO DISCUSS YOUR SPECIFIC SITUATION AND GET ANSWERS TO YOUR BURNING QUESTIONS. EMAIL – Russ@InsuranceByCastle.com or PHONE – 800-644-6443 extension 101.**

Chapter 5
The Buy and Hold Versus Flip Conundrum

Flipping has become a popular trend in real estate, as investors buy a home, renovate it, then attempt to quickly put it back on the market at a markup to make their profit. So many of the TV shows today paint a pretty picture of how easy it is to buy a fixer-upper, spend a few weeks and add a fresh coat of paint or two, and then flip the house and make outrageous profits. Oh, if it was that easy! Behind the scenes, the story couldn't be more untrue. These buildings take a lot of work. They take knowledge, commitment, and money. And, most importantly, they take a solid understanding of what is involved, especially from an insurance standpoint. Insurance companies will insure each of these differently. Most insurance companies that insure the long-term landlord will not insure the buy, fix, and flip rental. You need to make sure you inform your agent and get the proper protection.

You need to decide: Do you want to purchase a property and flip soon after purchase, or do you want to purchase a property and hold on it to for a long-term investment? Each option is work, but it's important to understand the ins and outs of how each works and decide what is best for you.

Also, even when investing in property, you can invest in a property that's ready to go, with few repairs, problems, etc., or one that has challenges, which will require you fixing up or using licensed contractors. Remember that it isn't as easy as it looks and, being knowledgeable will help you in your decision-making process. Oh, the choices!

Your financial well-being comes into play in making the right choice. As you move forward here think about your finances and how much you have to invest in your properties. Know what is needed to get these properties ready for purchase or rent. Renting properties often doesn't require as much upkeep in the beginning, but there are some cases where it might. Once you find a potential rental, a thorough inspection will reveal if, or how soon, the furnace, roof or electrical system, etc., will need repairs or replacement. In most cases these can be scheduled over the next few years, and defer the costs over many years. It's not always necessary to pay out the money in the beginning. However, go in knowing that in a few years you will need to invest in a new roof or new furnace or whatever that expense might be. Just because you don't invest in the beginning, doesn't mean you won't have to invest. Too many make that mistake. So, save and plan ahead.

Let's break it down.

Long-term rentals - Buying and holding onto property:

- Long-term rental properties provide passive income for years to come. Usually they do not require much day-to-day effort so the owner can pursue other interests. And as long as the units are rented, ongoing repetitive money will come in monthly. Nice!

- Regarding taxes, it can be a good investment. Dependent on the tax code in your area, you can depreciate over many years. Also, there might be other tax advantages, so check with experts and take the maximum allowances you can.
- Ongoing maintenance could be a positive or negative, depending on the building.
- You do run the risk of bad tenants who might be difficult to evict.
- In a number of areas here in California, the appreciation is significant and, by holding onto properties over the years, the equity increases as well.
- Insurance for buying and holding as a landlord is much more affordable than those that buy – fix - flip.

Flipping and Selling Immediately – Buying a property that needs some work done, fixing it up, and then selling as soon as possible

- One-time sale. You purchase, fix it up, and sell it— then it's done.
- In a lot of markets at this time, there are many foreclosures and pricing may be a great deal.
- You can realize a significant return on your investment after some initial work. But it's very risky in some neighborhoods.
- The repairs can often run higher than expected or there could be hidden repair work needed.
- You can take profits as soon as the property is sold. The profits from the flip can either be reinvested

into your next flipping project or kept and spent on anything you wish.

- At the current time, the demand for home purchases is increasing, so there is more potential to find the right properties.
- Holding costs are higher on a flip, because of the length of time it will take to sell verses rent. For selling, it can take time to get approved, do inspections, do all the paperwork involved, etc. We aren't talking years here, but again, that should come into consideration when you are planning your strategy.
- Insuring a rental property while renovations are being done and no tenant is living at the property requires a "course of construction" policy and these are not as competitive as the landlord policy. After the construction is complete, the property is "vacant" and this vacant insurance policy is not very competitive. The most affordable insurance policy for a landlord is one where the building is occupied with no renovations going on.

So, what is a "course of construction policy?" Sometimes known as a Builder's Risk Insurance policy, a Course of Construction policy protects owners, contractors, and subcontractors from losses such as flood, fire, theft, and vandalism on a property while it is under construction. Since this type of policy covers several different parties, it can be purchased by the owner, the contractor, or the project manager if one is involved in the project. They all are protected from lawsuits that may result when damages or losses occur.

All preferred landlord insurance policies require the building to be "occupied." If it is not "occupied," then parts of the coverage are void. The time that defines a building as "vacant" is not defined in the policy. Most insurance companies usually use a period of more than 60 days to be deemed as "vacant." If flipping a property, it is advisable to get a policy that covers "vacancies." It is more expensive, but worth it if there is a claim. (See Chapter 21 on Vacancies for more information.)

Now, there are other considerations as well. For example, say you invest in a flip, make the repairs to make it ready for the market, price it aggressively, and then nothing happens. It sits on the market. As you can imagine, you are then responsible for the monthly mortgage, insurance, interest, etc., and all costs involved. Not good...not good at all!

There are some good tips and a few alternative plans when you are looking at the property to purchase.

Plan A – Buy, fix up, and flip.

Plan B –Buy, fix and list for "xx" months and, if there are no good buyers, rent for "xx" months.

Plan C – Buy, fix up, list for "xx" months and, if there are no good buyers, rent long-term, and hold onto it.

Location can be an important consideration as well. Lower income neighborhoods, where properties are often lower costs to purchase, might take more money in fixing up and getting it ready to rent. Often times these properties haven't been taken care of, and that adds to your costs. Lower income areas also might have more Section 8 Rentals (See Chapter 33 on Section 8 Rentals). So, review carefully and take all of this into consideration.

Last, but certainly not least, there's the indisputable fact that rental properties can be income generators immediately. Traditional home investment where people live in their homes before selling them is more like parking money, similar to a bank account. Flipping nets more profit in a shorter period, but a lot of money is used in the renovation, making for thinner profit margins upon sale, whereas rentals immediately create revenue once tenants move in. This means that for a stable apartment building or other multi-family dwelling, pure profit can be recouped in a much faster period of time, but, more importantly, over a much a longer period of time as well. Just another consideration to think about.

HERE IS WHAT TO DO NEXT:
- **DECIDE ON 'BUY & FLIP' OR 'BUY & HOLD'**
- **DECIDE ON FIXER UPPERS OR READY TO GO**
- **FIND A LICENSED PROPERTY INSPECTOR TO ADD TO YOUR TEAM OF EXPERTS**
- **READ UP ON 'COURSE OF CONSTRUCTION' POLICIES**
- **CONTACT ME TO DISCUSS YOUR SPECIFIC SITUATION AND GET ANSWERS TO YOUR BURNING QUESTIONS. EMAIL – Russ@InsuranceByCastle.com or PHONE – 800-644-6443 extension 101.**

Chapter 6
To Self-Manage or Property Manage

A self-managed property is defined as a property where the owner takes care of everything. Whereas, hiring a property management company is where the property manager will handle the day-to-day activities and is sort of the "in between" between tenants and the owner. Some owners want to handle some of the tasks, with the property management company performing the balance of those tasks. And some want the property management company to do it all.

We have found that many owners choose to self-manage their own property. That's great, however, just know that you will be on call for any issues with the tenants contacting you directly. Depending on the tenant, some do not respect your time as much as they should. Of course, it's best to set boundaries early on (usually in the lease do's and don'ts), but even then, it can be challenging.

So, what is right for you? There are times when the decision is easy to make. The property might not be local or too far away to effectively manage. If you aren't able to collect rents, oversee repairs, be there for emergencies, etc., then the best way to go might be with a property management company.

Other scenarios include those where the property might just be too large. New to the business and taking on a 60- to 100-unit apartment complex would be challenging. And, unfortunately, you can imagine the stress that would bring.

There might be times where you just don't have the experience required. Yes, you can hire others to perform certain tasks, but that can get expensive. So, consider what your best options are and make these decisions early on before burn out occurs. And believe me, it will occur if you aren't set up properly.

Let's break it down further, so you can decide. A few advantages to self-managed property include:

- Saving money – All profits go to you – yeah! Management companies differ on what they require, but most want a percentage of rent, deposits, etc.
- More control – You will have a better understanding of what is happening at your property and can then quickly make decisions based on that. That knowledge is powerful.
- Great experience -- Especially in the beginning, by managing yourself, you gain a great deal of experience in how it all works. This can be priceless down the road as you add on more units.

Residential property managers act as a wall between the owner and the tenant with direct contact being limited. In some cases, the owner has NO contact with the tenant they only contact the property management company. The property management company finds the tenants, takes care of any issues or repairs, collects the rents, and pays the expenses (if the owner wants this much service).

There are several advantages to a management company, which include:

- They are already set up to manage residential rentals and they have everything that is needed already in place or close to it, which includes required paperwork. In the beginning, you probably do not have an office or staff, whereas normally a property management company usually does have one.
- Saves Time – It's obvious that with someone else running the day-to-day business activities, you are now free to work a full-time job if you want, look for other investments, or just enjoy more free time. You can be relaxed in the fact that they are experienced and taking care of things for you. Priceless!
- Less Stress – You will have tenants that are a piece of cake to deal with and then others that will try your every nerve. Having a property management company deal with that added stress allows you time to conduct business including finding new rentals, etc.
- If the property is over a certain number of units, the law requires you to have a property manager on site.
- The property management company has more expertise in the laws and practices for your state and that can be extremely beneficial. In addition

to the normal practices, things to consider include how much of a deposit you can require, rules on inspections, etc.

In my particular area, the tenant laws are changing every year. A property management company stays on top of all the changes so I don't have to. Some owners, who do not use a property management company, might not be up to date on all the laws, which can lead to problems.

An apartment building with over 16 units is required by law to have a property manager living on the premises in my area of California. Even if the landlord wants to manage this size of a building, he must have an onsite manager by law.

It should also be noted that it is imperative to review the laws and government codes for your area dealing with property management. There can be laws on safety issues, insurance, taxes, etc., that you might not be aware of.

Many states, such as California, also require property managers to hold a real estate broker's license or be employed by someone who does. Additionally, ongoing educational training and licensing might be involved. Once again, discuss this openly with the company you wish to hire, in addition to doing your research or talking to those more knowledgeable.

HERE IS WHAT TO DO NEXT:

- DECIDE ON SELF MANAGED OR PROPERTY MANAGEEMENT COMPANIES
- FAMILARIZE YOURSELF WITH LOCAL LAWS AND CODES FOR PROPERTY MANAGEMENT
- CONTACT ME TO DISCUSS YOUR SPECIFIC SITUATION AND GET ANSWERS TO YOUR BURNING QUESTIONS. EMAIL – Russ@InsuranceByCastle.com or PHONE – 800-644-6443 extension 101.

Part 3

It's A Business – Manage It Well and Reap the Rewards

Chapter 7
Expert Tips on First Impression

As a landlord, one of your primary responsibilities is ensuring that you provide tenants with a safe, quality space in which to live. In return for a safe, quality space you receive a monthly income through rent, and, if they are particularly good tenants, they'll do this with a minimum amount of trouble to you. The best way to find these tenants is to have your property highlight its assets. This is not only for potential renters, but also for all others including the insurance inspectors.

Insurance inspections will often take place at various times throughout the rental process. You want the inspector to be satisfied that everything is up-to-date and in the best possible condition. Most insurance companies will inspect the location once the policy is written and then every few years.

When you think about it, if you were the insurance company, would you want to insure a property that was not well maintained? Probably not. In some cases, you would think this property was a claim waiting to happen and that's the last thing the insurance company and the landlord want to happen.

Here are a few things an insurance inspector might be reviewing:

1. Is the location what was represented on the application from the insurance agent? Is the address correct?

2. Does it look like it was built when it was stated on the application?
3. Is the square footage and number of units aligned with what was on the application?
4. Is the housekeeping in good order? For example, is the driveway free of potholes just begging for a claim? Are the trees well maintained or do they hang on the roof (causing more roof damage and potentially leaks)?
5. Are the rental units occupied or vacant? Preferred insurance policies will only allow a certain percentage (20-35%) of vacancies at a time. If vacant, there will be more damage in the event of a water leak, or someone damaging the building, potentially without being noticed for some time. (See Chapter 21 on "Vacant" properties).

All of these items are to help the owner as much as they help prevent a claim. Poor housekeeping also reflects on the type of tenant and how the property is treated as well as the probability of a claim.

Let's talk about the property itself. Before you can rent, normally you will paint and perform any necessary repairs to get your property ready.

Other things to consider when updating the property:

- Choose timeless and durable updates. While it may be tempting to have the latest home decorating trends, it's best to keep your décor classic and timeless. Before you invest in new light fixtures or flooring, ask yourself, "Will this still look nice 5 or 10 years from now?" Go for neutral colors and durable, easy-to-clean finishes.

- Decide on carpeting. Do you want to replace the carpet with each tenant if needed, or would a light-colored wood or ceramic tile work best? Though it may cost slightly more than installing carpet, it may not ever have to be replaced. In a worst-case scenario, if a tenant were to drop something heavy on the flooring, it could be easy to repair the small damaged area instead of re-carpeting the entire room. Also, light-colored wood or ceramic tile helps to make the space look bigger when showing the property for rent. And finally, for those with pets, this could be a big benefit over carpets.

- Keep the heating and cooling systems updated, and maintained You may notice an undesirable odor coming from the air conditioning unit. This could be dirty or clogged coils, which may not only create the undesirable odor, but restrict air flow. This causes the unit to work harder, making it not only less efficient, but shortening its life span as well. Be sure to have your handyman change the air filter in the unit at least 2-3 times per year to help prevent this condition. Chances are very good that your tenant is not going to bother with replacing air filters.

- Enhance the landscaping. Planting perennials and hardscaping will take little effort, but make a huge difference. Hardscaping is the practice of laying out harder materials in the yard space. This includes patios, decks, fire pits, rock gardens, and other installations that don't use plants. With the right allotment of space and design, a hardscaped yard can look incredibly attractive. In the backyard, this can also be quite practical, as decks and fire pits have obvious utility for tenants. Because you're taking up more space with harder materials like stone, wood, or concrete, the amount of maintenance you have to put into the environment is minimized.

- Make the entrance appealing – An inexpensive, yet worthwhile investment, is making the front of the house or apartment appealing. Even changes to the front door can make a huge difference. Consider a new door if needed, quality mailboxes, windows that work and look good, etc. In some areas that are prone to natural disasters, also consider weather-related windows and if they would add value to your property. This will be a renter's first impression and first impressions go a long way.

- Have a maintenance schedule for routine cleaning of the gutters, trimming the shrubs, trees and keeping debris off the building, as well as other routine items.

- Consider adding artificial grass. It has a reputation for being eco-friendly because it doesn't need water, fertilizer, or mowing. Artificial grass is one of the cheapest, long-term solutions to having a presentable lawn that requires the absolute lowest standard of maintenance. It can be a little more expensive with the initial installation, and you definitely don't want to consider this for massive, sprawling fields. In addition, the newest generation of artificial grass often looks good enough to fool us into thinking it's real.

- Replace baseboards as needed since scuffed or damaged baseboards are easy and economical to replace.
- Changing knobs and handles is an easy way to update your property. Replace old doorknobs and kitchen cabinet handles with more modern ones.
- Document the repairs and upgrades to the property. Seems like a no-brainer, but this helps prove you are ahead of the game and doing what is best for you and you tenants.
- Do a thorough cleaning or hire a company to do that for you. Pay special attention to dust on ceiling fans, furnace vents and other areas that aren't usually included in the day-to-day cleaning of the units.

NOTE: When an insurance company has an inspector report on the building, they will send the owner a report listing requirements of repairs and other suggestions. Make sure to respond and fix those items needed. If you do not, you will not be able to keep the preferred insurance company.

Another thing you can do that we recommend is to ask for feedback from your tenants about what they like and don't like about the property. Most tenants are more than willing to provide opinions on what they think should be updated or replaced. Put yourself in the shoes of a tenant—what would you want fixed if you were living there? But keep in mind you, the landlord, make the decisions—not your tenants.

Finally know that everyone's tastes differ. You can tell from the neighborhood often times what is most acceptable in paint colors, landscaping, etc. Try not to stand out too much. You don't want to be the neighbor with the bright yellow house and landscaping that is the talk of the town.

<u>HERE IS WHAT TO DO NEXT:</u>
- **CONSIDER GIVING ALL YOUR PROPERTIES AN UPDATE TO IMPROVE CURB APPEAL**
- **CREATE A MAINTENANCE SCHEDULE FOR YOUR STRATEGIC MAINTENACE PARTNER**
- **ADD A GOOD CLEANING COMPANY TO YOUR EXPERTS TEAM**
- **CCONTACT ME TO DISCUSS YOUR SPECIFIC SITUATION AND GET ANSWERS TO YOUR BURNING QUESTIONS. EMAIL – <u>Russ@InsuranceByCastle.com</u> or PHONE – 800-644-6443 extension 101.**

Chapter 8
Pets & Your Tenants

Having animals in your property is guaranteed to be one of the areas you need to address right from the start. Let's talk pros and cons to help you make better decisions.

Some residential rental owners don't like to have dogs, cats or any pets. Pets usually mean more of the following:

- Wear and tear on the rental unit. In addition to carpets needing replacement sooner, the larger animals will require more frequent painting of walls between tenants and other tasks as well.
- Potential for damage due to the animal, which includes damage to both the inside and outside of the property.
- Issues with neighbors. You may receive complaints from neighbors and other tenant's due to noise, smell, messes, and property destruction. Also, if you have an aggressive pet (one that bites) that can be an immediate problem.
- In multiple unit rentals, it's possible to lose tenants due to another tenant's pets. If one tenant is too inconvenienced, and they feel the situation won't change, they are likely to move to a better environment. You obviously want to resolve matters prior to that.

So, let's talk more about what all is involved with tenants and their pets. First of all, you want to have a pet policy that includes the dos and don'ts as part of the lease. This way all tenants know the rules and can make their decisions based upon them. Some of the items on the policy include noise issues, cleanup after the pet, how many animals are allowed per unit, the size of the pets allowed (i.e., up to 20 lbs.,) etc. Openly discuss your policy with those looking at your rentals.

In the agreement, other things can be addressed as well such as keeping pets up to date with shots and licenses. It can also be added that all pets be properly groomed and cared for and what steps you will take if it is discovered this is not taking place as you don't want problems with neighbors or city and health officials.

Make sure the lease asks for a larger security deposit to cover any additional expenses when the tenant moves out. Also, know your pet policy is more than dogs and cats. You might want to address whether you allow snakes, birds, ferrets, or other animals.

One obvious sign of having pets is the odor that can come with having them. Always have your property smelling good. Dog and animal smells will immediately present a problem, and many potential renters will walk away from the unit before they give it a second look. This is especially true for those who aren't pet owners. But when you think about it, would you want to stay at a place where the smell is bad enough to notice. You'd always be concerned about the effect this might have on your living conditions, especially if you have any health issues. Bottom line, take care of this now and have steps in place for the future as well.

Some try and mask the smell with candles, Febreze, baking cookies when it's time to show the unit, etc. Don't. Potential tenants will think more could be going on in addition to the odors that are so obvious.

Now there can be an upside to allowing pets. Generally, in regard to renters, pet owners tend to stay longer as it is often difficult to find a unit that meets all the needs of the tenant and animal, so that can be a plus.

Make sure to check with your insurance company regarding animal coverage and liability amounts. See if they specify types and breeds of animals that are disallowed or violate the insurance coverage. The types and breeds of animals that may violate coverage are written as exclusions in the lease or rental agreement.

There are some instances where the laws favor pet owners. For example, Fair Housing laws can require the allowance of pets when renting to someone who is disabled and requires the use of a service animal, even if you have a "no pet policy." In California and other states, laws are also changing to allow renters to have a "comfort animal" and, therefore, the landlord must allow the pet.

The definition of "comfort animals" is often changing as well. Be sure to regularly check with local and state laws regarding service and comfort animals. Even though this is the law, most preferred insurance companies have a list of some breeds that are excluded due to claims history (primarily biting).

HERE IS WHAT TO DO NEXT:

- **DECIDE YOU WANT TO DEAL WITH PETS OR NOT**
- **ADOPT A PET POLICY**
- **INCREASE YOUR SECURITY DEPOSIT FOR FOLKS WITH PETS**
- **CONTACT ME TO DISCUSS YOUR SPECIFIC SITUATION AND GET ANSWERS TO YOUR BURNING QUESTIONS. EMAIL – Russ@InsuranceByCastle.com or PHONE – 800-644-6443 extension 101.**

Chapter 9
Why Courts Like Tenants More Than Landlords

In many claims, the courts rule in favor of the tenant over the landlord as many courts look at the tenant as the victim. In the court's eyes, the landlord is a "well established" person that has assets and insurance to help with the claim. In most cases, the tenant does not have much in the way of assets and usually has no renter's insurance. This is just something you should know and acknowledge. Of course, that is not always the case. But again, our hope throughout this book is to prepare you for those unknowns.

Although the benefit of the doubt often goes to the tenant or visitor and not the owner, there are general guidelines in place. Liability cases are often determined by who was in control of the property, so persons occupying the property can be held responsible for claims. Even if a person is occupying without an owner's knowledge or permission, they can sometimes be held responsible for injuries. Since there is no foolproof means of knowing something like this ahead of time, having your tenant secure Renter's Insurance and you having enough protection is essential. We suggest at least $300,000 or more of liability insurance on these renter's policies.

There are circumstances where the owner will be seen at fault in the event of an injury. Let's say the property is rented under dangerous conditions, not meeting codes, or rented in an attempt to cover up potential hazards.

The owner will certainly be found at fault. Therefore, it is important for the owner to ensure that all properties are rented under safe conditions and up to all standards and codes for the area. While this should be obvious and goes without saying, some people will often try to cut corners or cover up hazards. While cutting corners when it comes to code or safety may save money in the short term, it can lead to larger problems in the long run if claims or injuries come about as a result. Plus, you just don't want that added stress of not doing things right.

You want to be known as an ethical and trustworthy landlord. Even one incident can damage your reputation. We highly recommend always putting your best foot forward and taking care of any problems as soon as they arise.

Let's discuss some areas of concern to watch for. One example is that an owner can be held responsible for an injury that occurs in the common area of an apartment building as these areas are generally considered the owner's responsibility. These areas include walkways, stairs, etc. You can take steps to ensure these common areas are well maintained and won't cause injury.

Of additional note here is the importance of having good tenants. If you do a good job of screening, checking references, background checks, etc., plus follow-up your tenant checklist you can often weed out those tenants who are a claim away. There are those tenants that will take advantages of situations for their own profits. You want to avoid these types of tenants at all costs.

So, in addition to making sure the properties are in good condition and safe, you should carry enough insurance to not only fix the building and cover the loss of rents, but also enough liability insurance to cover most claims. Liability insurance is very inexpensive considering the amount of damages the landlord could have to pay. Plus, the liability portion of the policy should also pay for the legal fees to defend the claim. In a number of instances, the legal fees were the major expense.

There is no right or wrong amount of liability insurance. The total limit is up to the owner. Think about what makes you feel safe and secure and not fearful of a claim. In the event of a claim, what amount of liability insurance would cover most claims? You do not want to be "insurance poor," but rather have enough to pay these claims. If the limit is not enough, then the owner is paying the balance out of pocket (and after-tax dollars as well).

Let's also discuss tenants and their rights. The bottom line is, there are almost always going to be some landlord/tenant problems to be dealt with. Tenants should know their rights, as well as their responsibilities. Sometimes, things are the responsibility of the tenant and not the landlord.

The following are examples of some tenant landlord problems and suggestions on how they may best be dealt with:

- **Water Leaks** – Most problems can wait until normal working hours before you contact the landlord. However, a major water leak can have devastating effects and cause notable damage in a relatively short period of time. It is usually the tenant's responsibility to ensure that problems with the property do not escalate. Calling the landlord immediately about such problems can help ensure you are not held responsible.

- **Broken Smoke Detectors** – In most states, smoke detectors are required in rental units, and landlords are responsible to ensure they do indeed exist in good working order. However, before a tenant should call the landlord in the middle of the night, a good tenant will ensure the problem isn't something as simple as a dead battery. And these calls are best made during working hours obviously.

- **Plumbing Problems** – The landlord is responsible for ensuring the plumbing in your unit is proper and up to code. However, tenants should be able to fix a clogged sink or toilet. If the problem persists though, the landlord should be advised.

- **Structurally Deficient Floors, Stairways, or Roofs** – Most states have laws mandating the landlord maintains their rental property in a structurally sound condition. This means if a tenant's roof is leaking, their floor cracked and rotting, or the stairs leading to their apartment are loose and wobbly, tenants should contact their landlord immediately.

- **Heating and Cooling Systems** – You will probably find your state mandates a minimum indoor temperature during the winter months. If problems arise and the heat or air conditioning is not operating correctly, especially on extremely cold or hot days, tenants should contact their landlord immediately.

- **Pest Control** –If rodents or insects are infesting an apartment or home, it's the landlord's responsibility to provide adequate extermination service. However, if the tenant's living habits are the cause of the issue, (for example lack of adequate housekeeping or cleaning) the tenants might be responsible.

HERE IS WHAT TO DO NEXT:

- **LOOK INTO A GOOD LIABILITY POLICY**
- **MAKE SURE YOUR PROPERTIES ARE IN GOOD CONDITION AND SAFE**
- **CONTACT ME TO DISCUSS YOUR SPECIFIC SITUATION AND GET ANSWERS TO YOUR BURNING QUESTIONS. EMAIL – Russ@InsuranceByCastle.com or PHONE – 800-644-6443 extension 101.**

Chapter 10
11 Insider Secrets to Saving on Your Rental and More

Making more money—who doesn't want that right? There are so many ways to make your business profitable, many you learn from experience. But these should help as well.

Here are some of the best ways to save on owning residential rentals:

1. Start small and build your way to more rentals. Learn while you are small and any mistakes will also be smaller. Once you have a good grasp of what you want in residential real estate, then start increasing the number of rentals.

2. The larger you get; the more economies of scale are available. For example, a repair contractor will give you a better rate if they know you have multiple rentals versus one rental. Your gardener will give you a better rate with more properties. If you are using a property management firm, they will give you a better rate with the more rentals you place with them. See where we are going here? A great way to save money is to reward those you work with by growing and including them in your growth. Not only will they give you a better rate, but often times they are more dedicated to you.

3. Insurance premiums will also be reduced if you have multiple locations. It is called the "multiple building discount." The insurance company knows

the likelihood of one claim happening on multiple locations is small and thus will reduce the cost for this exposure.

4. Your lender will be very happy to get a better deal if you are increasing the number of rentals and thus the size of the loan. In some cases, you'll get even a lower interest rate.

5. Finding tenants can possibly be better the more units you have because of the sources you acquire over the years. This, in turn, will mean you have units available more often so these sources will turn to you before other possible owners.

6. Save on the cost of upkeep and other expenses by keeping the units well maintained and the grounds looking good. In the long run, you will get better rents as well as attract better tenants. Also, when tenants see the landlord working on the maintenance of their property and taking good care of it, they are more likely to do the same.

7. Make extra money on rentals when you allow pets on your properties. Usually you can collect a fee for pets on top of increased rents. Now, you don't want to make this fee too expensive, but even a small amount will increase your profits. Multiple that by the number of units you own and you can easily see a difference in profits. Plus, you can often have options for multiple pets so those pet lovers will pay more per pet. Of course, you want to set limits. Like how the airlines started adding baggage charges a few years ago that resulted in billions of extra dollars. Additionally, pet-friendly rentals are usually in high demand and often those with pets won't want to

vacate because of fear of finding another rental where they can keep their pets. However, take into consideration the effects of having pets on your property that we have discussed previously. Make sure the pros outweigh the cons.

8. Keep vacancies to a minimum. One way to do that too is to allow residents to upgrade their properties. They will feel more at home with their favorite paint and updated appliances.

9. Protect your vacancies. Have heavy-duty locks, alarms, exterior lights, etc. Keep the landscaping in good condition so it's easy to see all doors and windows. (This is good to do even without a vacancy.)

10. Install energy efficient appliances. Some tenants, especially today, will pay more to be environmentally friendly. Not only that, but the monthly costs are less. Even though it might cost more initially, they can pay for themselves fairly quickly.

11. You can also save money by doing maintenance and upkeep yourself. Of course, only you can decide if you want to be involved or not. Just know that the more you do the more money you save.

Also, note when hiring the type of work required will dictate how much you spend. You can hire a handyman for tasks that are less complicated and need less experience. However, for some tasks it's imperative to pay someone who is skilled and experienced such as a licensed professional contractor or electrician.

Some things might be best done by a handyman:

- Painting
- Small electrical work
- Minor repairs
- Tiling
- Sheetrock
- Clogged toilets and drains
- Rekeying when tenants move out
- Landscaping

Some things you should ALWAYS hire a professional contractor for:

- Major electrical work
- Installing windows
- Cabinet work (other than minor repairs)
- Major plumbing
- Central heating and air conditioning replacement or repairs
- Roofing
- Any major structural work

HERE IS WHAT TO DO NEXT:

- **LOOK FOR WAYS TO SAVE MONEY ON YOUR INVESTMENTS**
- **DISCUSS GOALS AND COMMITMENTS WITH YOUR TEAM OF EXPERTS**
- **CONSIDER INVESTING IN SECURITY SYSTEMS FOR YOUR RENTALS**
- **CONTACT ME TO DISCUSS YOUR SPECIFIC SITUATION AND GET ANSWERS TO YOUR BURNING QUESTIONS. EMAIL – Russ@InsuranceByCastle.com or PHONE – 800-644-6443 extension 101.**

Chapter 11
Tenants are Not Your Friends

When it comes to being a landlord, keep it professional. You can have a friendly relationship with your tenants, which is strongly encouraged, but you need to treat them as your tenants. In other words, like owning a company or in management, your employees are not your best friends—they are your employees and having boundaries is important.

Now we encourage good relationships and doing all you can to make that happen as, then, things will go smoother. But again, set your boundaries. Let your tenants know that calling at midnight for something that could be done in the morning is discouraged. Or coming to you to "bend the rules just this once" to let more people stay with them, can lead to problems down the road. Let them know you are on their side, but you, as a business owner, need to keep things running smoothly. Believe us, if you cave just once, it will be expected each and every time and then you turn into the "bad guy" when you put your foot down.

You can be forthright with them and let them know bending the rules would mean you'd have to do the same for all your tenants.

Now go in knowing that you get to decide what type of tenants you want. For example, does the area in which you want property have more single moms or is it more inclined toward married couples. What is the age of the tenants normally? Is it a younger crowd of millennials or more middle-aged residents?

Why is this important? The living arrangements and challenges you might face differ depending on the demographics of your tenants. The younger crowd can be great tenants. However, they might have more late-night parties and guests. Middle-aged families can also be great tenants, but with younger children, their focus might be on the schools in the area and as their children grow and reach driving age, they might require more parking. It's just important to know what your target renter looks like. With that in mind, you can make it a win/win for all. Knowing that they might have more late-night parties, you can have your agreement define the rules more aggressively and be crystal clear on areas that might cause concern. Knowing schools are important; you can verify the quality of nearby schools and add that in the marketing and listings.

Additionally, with this information, you can also know what you can charge. A struggling college student might not be able to pay as much as a middle-class family with two kids. By recognizing this, you can be better prepared to address late payments and consequences and even the amount of rent you can charge.

So, with that knowledge in hand, set up your rules and regulations and make sure all tenants comply. Do your research and make sure these are good tenants for your unit, starting with turning in a completed application. Explain the rules of your units so they understand the dos and don'ts. If they do not comply, then you need to take appropriate action. If you have a property management firm handling this, they can take over, but make sure they keep you in the loop on what is happening.

Finally, we recommend rewarding good tenants. Let them know you appreciate their timely rent payments and keeping the unit in good shape. Keep the line of communication open so they feel that they can come to you with issues.

HERE IS WHAT TO DO NEXT:

- **BE FRIENDLY AND CORDIAL WITH YOUR TENANTS BUT REMEMBER THIS IS A BUSINESS**
- **DON'T BEND THE RULES**
- **CONTACT ME TO DISCUSS YOUR SPECIFIC SITUATION AND GET ANSWERS TO YOUR BURNING QUESTIONS. EMAIL – Russ@InsuranceByCastle.com or PHONE – 800-644-6443 extension 101.**

Chapter 12
Rental Agreements Musts

A rental agreement provides the rules to be followed by tenants and clearly states the dos and don'ts that you expect. As a legal contract, it also is packed full of information that both the landlords and tenants need to know. And, it should meet all applicable laws for your area.

The size of the agreement varies. It is just necessary to include everything that is important to you and the successful of your business.

Know that, as you gain experience, you can add to your agreements. Often times landlords will update their agreements once certain situations occur. Say they had some challenges with a previous tenant. Because of what transpired, they now add additional language to their agreement that would cover this particular situation.

There are many resources that can help with the contract, rules and what you can and can't do with regard to your tenants. Take the time to familiarize yourself with these. Also, note that we regularly blog and add social media postings frequently on this topic, so look to us for updated advice.

Some items your contract should include:

- Name of tenant(s) and all adults residing in the unit
- Address of the unit
- Parking (if specified spot) and number of spaces

- Guests and how long they can stay without being on the lease
- Limit of people living in the unit (including guests)
- Monthly rent and when payments are due
- Method of rental payment
- What types of payments do you take (checks, online payments, etc.)?
- The time period before rent is considered to be late
- The charge if a check bounces
- What the increase in rents will be each year or if It will increase each year
- The deposit amount, terms for when it is due, when and how it would be returned when they move out
- What qualifies as deductions from the deposit
- Any rules or procedures that tenants need to know when moving out (such as should they turn off the electricity, etc.)
- Who is responsible for which utilities
- The term of the lease and, if an option for extending the term is available
- The rules regarding noise and quiet times
- How repairs and maintenance will be handled. Be very clear on this. The more instructions you provide, the easier it is when repairs need to be made
- Entry by the owner and when and how much notice will be given
- Actions not acceptable in the unit (legal or Illegal)
- Subletting (if permitted or not)
- If a dispute occurs, who pays the legal fees
- All the references and background checks that will be required

- Pertinent laws in your area for tenant or landlord

There are also some things that cannot legally be in a rental agreement. One example might be reference to tenant's due to race, sex, etc. It is best to review your local guidelines to ensure you are doing everything right.

Keep all your agreements protected and in a safe place. It's good to tell your business associates or others where all your agreements are kept as well. Say you were disabled or not able to run your business, having someone know where everything is kept can be a real benefit. Disaster preparedness is always a good idea.

HERE IS WHAT TO DO NEXT:
- **SUBSCRIBE TO OUR BLOG**
- **FAMILARIZE YOURSELF RENTAL AGREEMENT REQUIREMENTS**
- **DRAFT YOUR TENANT AGREEMENT**
- **CONTACT ME TO DISCUSS YOUR SPECIFIC SITUATION AND GET ANSWERS TO YOUR BURNING QUESTIONS. EMAIL – Russ@InsuranceByCastle.com or PHONE – 800-644-6443 extension 101.**

Chapter 13
Landlord Do's & Don'ts with Tenants

We have pointed out what makes an ideal tenant throughout the book, but we wanted to break it down further.

There should be a list of the rules you abide by and these rules will apply with every tenant. It is important that you treat ALL prospective tenants, tenants, and former tenants the same; don't play favorites.

Just as important as the rules are what happens if the rules are broken. Do you give a few warnings and then take action? And what exact action will you take? It's always easier to enforce rules when you have made them clear on what happens.

Most of these rules are part of the lease. Some of the main rules are:

- What are tenants supposed to do when they have any problems in their rentals?
- Who and how do they contact with issues or concerns
- How to handle a difficulty with another tenant(s)
- If a pool, the rules and regulations of the pool
- If a laundry facility is shared with other tenants, what are the rules and regulations?
- What rules pertain to noise and "quiet hours"? What happens when you abuse these requirements? Do you have warnings?

- What are the rules pertaining to actions in the units? What happens if you are caught doing something illegal?
- Can you sublet your apartment? Any rules that need to be followed regarding that?
- If you have pets, what rules apply?
- Can they update their unit? Is so, what is allowed and what is not?

Once you gain a little experience as a landlord, you will be more knowledgeable on rules that are important to you and you can add to this list. Just don't make it too difficult for your tenants to follow. But again, you, as the landlord, set the rules and regulations.

Now let's discuss the initial steps in leasing your unit. When starting the leasing of a unit, make sure the first step is a phone interview. From the minute they answer the phone, consider the interview to have begun and don't just focus on the answers to your questions, but on the overall call and how it went. If you have any doubts that something is wrong, go with your gut and ask more questions or decide against them as tenants. You'll soon get to where this is standard procedure. If they pass this test, then make sure to meet the prospective tenant at the unit and show them the site. Most landlords know there are some things you can and can't ask. For example, you can't ask them their age, religious beliefs, ethnic background, or sexual preferences. Set a procedure and do the same procedure each and every time. You are discriminating if you vary from one person to the next.

Run credit and criminal checks. Ask for personal references and prior landlords to check as well.

HERE IS WHAT TO DO NEXT:

- **TREAT ALL PROSPECTIVE TENANTS, TENANTS, AND FORMER TENANTS THE SAME**
- **DRAFT YOUR TENANT INTERVIEW PROCESS**
- **RUN TENANT CREDIT CHECKS**
- **RUN TENANT CRIMINAL CHECKS**
- **LEARN WHAT YOU CAN AND CAN'T ASK DURING AN INTERVIEW**
- **CONTACT ME TO DISCUSS YOUR SPECIFIC SITUATION AND GET ANSWERS TO YOUR BURNING QUESTIONS. EMAIL – Russ@InsuranceByCastle.com or PHONE – 800-644-6443 extension 101.**

Chapter 14
What Type of Tenant Do You Want

The first rule is that every tenant signs an agreement. It may seem like a no-brainer, but there are many who make this mistake so we want to address it. All interested tenants should complete a rental agreement. That goes for friends, family, friends of friends, aunts, cousins, nephews, etc. Nothing can destroy a great relationship faster than having something go wrong in this area. So, make it a practice that everyone does this and avoid headaches that are sure to follow if you don't.

When you decide to become a landlord, it's imperative to consider this a business. And as a business, legal forms need to be completed. And, they need to be completed each and every time. There...we said it! Now we cover rental agreements in more detail in other chapters, but for these purposes know it always needs to be done.

In addition to the rental agreement, a comprehensive tenant screening including a credit and background check is always a good idea. You can find out everything you may need or want to know about a potential tenant from a credit and/or background check. You will learn about their credit rating, late payment history, criminal activities, legal arbitrations, etc., from a simple credit and background check. When you think about it, if you rent without doing a credit check, you could easily end up with someone who makes it a practice of not paying and getting evicted.

Sad to say, but there are some who know the system and look for opportunities where landlords are naïve or too busy to check and soon the trouble begins. You don't want that to happen to you. You would be surprised how often we see tenants with numerous evictions on their record who have made it a practice of living rent-free. This credit check will ensure you aren't added to that list.

Some might not have a lot of credit, which doesn't necessarily mean they wouldn't be good tenants. Do your due diligence in other areas to get a better idea on this tenant.

For the background check, don't you want to know your tenant's history, especially if it's really bad? Someone who has multiple convictions for burglary or abuse might not be the best tenant for your family-friendly apartments. Remember, it is your duty to protect your tenants so always find out their history in advance. Always keep in mind that a tenant's problems somehow seem to become a landlord's challenges, so make sure you are renting only to those you can trust and who don't come with a ton of baggage. Remember if something were to happen on your property, you can become liable for it. So, proceed accordingly.

You can also ask for references. Many landlords ask, but don't follow-up thinking if they are giving them to me, they must be okay. Not the way to do it. You should ask for references and follow-up on all those references. And don't be shy in asking questions that will give you a better idea of these tenants. You can often talk to previous landlords as well. Consider questions such as: Did they pay on time? Did they keep the rental in good condition? Did you have any problems with noise or too many parties? Anything else you feel we should know?

I think the best question for a prior landlord, "Would you rent to them today if you had a vacancy?" This is a great question. If they hesitate at all, that is a telling of some issue the tenant had with this prior landlord.

You also want to check on their employment. Are they working where they say they are working? Often times you can ask for a recent pay stub or tax records to find this out. If the pay stub is from 5 years ago, you might want to look further into it. Your tenant might think you won't notice, but obviously, you will want to.

For all the above, let your tenant know you are following up. Normally they give you the green light immediately, but again, get permission. They need to know you are doing all this checking on them.

We know some landlords are so eager to fill their vacancies that they fear that asking for all these will scare away prospects. Bottom line—it doesn't. If the tenants looking at your properties are serious, they know this comes with the territory and are happy to do so. Having them fill out agreements saves you from the "tire-kickers" or those just trying to price shop.

We also feel it's important to ask for an application fee. This again weeds out those who are just looking. They can take up valuable time and often have no intention of living in your apartments. Some might have another apartment in mind and want to know if they are getting a good deal with that one. You can imagine what a waste of time that is. With the application fee, you can decide whether or not it's refundable. Normally it's a good idea to use the application fee towards the deposit. But check your state to see if there are any rules or regulations regarding this.

All of this paperwork is one of the most IMPORTANT parts of being a landlord. This contract will be what you need if you ever go to court. It explains the do's and don'ts for the tenants. It explains when rent will be collected and the move in and move-out procedures. It explains all the ins and outs of renting and protects you if something were to go amiss.

We recommend having a checklist and following that checklist each and every time. The paperwork will also spell out that you are checking the references they list, checking the prior rentals, and running background plus criminal check. All we have stated above can be on this checklist so it's more of a "to do" list for you and, with it, you don't need to worry you are forgetting something important.

With your checklist and agreements, make sure that in addition to the screening of tenants and move in procedures, and rules while occupying your unit, you also cover the "moving out" procedures. Make it crystal clear what happens, how they get their deposit back, etc. Keep in mind normal wear and tear on units can be expected and shouldn't be penalized. Also, what steps must the tenants complete? For example, is it the tenant's responsibility to get the carpets professionally cleaned or not?

We know of a recent case where the tenants were not given any guidelines for moving out and got penalized for turning off the electricity the day they moved. The landlord wanted them to keep it on three days so they could get in and clean, etc. However, nowhere was this written or stated, so the tenant was able to fight it. But the bottom line was it caused undue stress on everyone because the rules weren't clearly stated.

Deposits are normally due within 20 to 60 days dependent on your state. However, why wait? After a good inspection, reward your good tenants by giving them their deposits back soon. They will certainly appreciate that and be more willing to tell others what a great experience they had with you.

Make sure all the items we have listed in this book are part of the application. Any shortcuts or not making your application as complete as possible will hurt you in the long run. It pays to be thorough.

We suggest either working with the local rental association (or state association) to get the best rental applications. They are the most complete and in depth. They cover most, if not all, areas you will want to address.

HERE IS WHAT TO DO NEXT:

- DRAFT AND PUBLISH YOUR TENANT AGREEMENT
- CREATE YOUR TEANT SCREENING PROCESS
- ASK FOR AND FOLLOW UP ON ALL REFERENCES
- IMPLEMENT AN APPLICATION FEE
- DRAFT 'MOVE IN' AND 'MOVE OUT' PROCEEDURES
- CONTACT ME TO DISCUSS YOUR SPECIFIC SITUATION AND GET ANSWERS TO YOUR BURNING QUESTIONS. EMAIL – Russ@InsuranceByCastle.com or PHONE – 800-644-6443 extension 101.

Chapter 15
Are Section 8 Tenants Right for You?

"Section 8" dates back to the Housing Act of 1937. It is the Department of Housing and Urban Development (HUD) subsidized housing program for lower income families. These are tenants that qualify for financial help from the government. The good news for landlords is that it can be a great way to keep your apartments full. The bad news is it often involves more paperwork and government involvement, including more frequent inspections, and the tenants might not be as reliable of a tenant as others.

The tenant's financial situation determines how much payment will be received and several things are taken into consideration including the tenant's finances, whether or not they are employed, how many dependents they have, any medical issues, and other factors.

The voucher program is the most popular. These vouchers are normally for one- to three-bedroom properties. Also of note is that there are specific guidelines for the sizes of the rooms. This is something you want to check on prior to investing. Rent is pre-set and normally and you want to be sure that this rate works for you. Whereas with your own apartments you can set the rates, the case might not be the same here.

However, it isn't all good. Let's discuss some of the pros and cons of having Section 8 tenants.

Pros

- The rent is guaranteed every month. There are fewer worries about receiving payment on time and all the many excuses for non-payment. (Really your grandmother passed away again and you had to go visit?)
- Often times the rent is higher than you would receive from other units.
- This tenant generally stays longer. The process to move and get the Section 8 approval for the tenant in another location is a long process
- There are a number of senior tenants that are Section 8 and might not have any issues for you as the landlord

Cons

- Section 8 tenants can sometimes not take as much pride in their occupancy as other tenants. Therefore, they might not take as good of care of the rental unit. Often, they don't take the necessary steps needed to prevent problems, such as calling the landlord for faucets not working, not maintaining proper upkeep of the house, etc.
- It can be hard to get insurance as most preferred insurance companies won't insure if there are Section 8 tenants or they will only insure up to 10-15% of the units in a building.
- There are requirements the landlord needs to meet in order to get Section 8 tenants. Ongoing benchmarks are required to keep everything current.

- If there is an eviction, you have one more layer you need to work through and this sometimes means a longer timeframe for eviction.
- There will be more government involvement and regulations.
- If something is found to be wrong with the unit, it usually must be fixed prior to tenants moving in. These units are inspected and quite often lists provided on what must be done for compliance. You want your unit in the best shape possible anyway, so we don't see this as a negative, but something more to be aware of.

HERE IS WHAT TO DO NEXT:

- **DECIDE IF YOU'RE INTERESTED IN SECTION 8 TENANTS**
- **WEIGH OUT THE PROS AND CONS OF SECTION 8 TENANTS**
- **CONTACT ME TO DISCUSS YOUR SPECIFIC SITUATION AND GET ANSWERS TO YOUR BURNING QUESTIONS. EMAIL – Russ@InsuranceByCastle.com or PHONE – 800-644-6443 extension 101.**

Chapter 16
Best Time of the Year to Get a Tenant

When renting residential properties, there is a time of the year that is better than any other. I am not saying you can't rent throughout the year. However, believe it or not, March 31 is the magical anniversary date. Most tenants do not like to move during the holidays or bad weather, and this seems to fit with most schedules.

Lease expiration dates are important. You truly want to time them for when people are most likely to look. Those with a lease are usually looking to move at the end of the school year and start apartment hunting in April, and current tenants, with school-age children, generally don't want to move until summer. Therefore, during this end of March time frame, it is more likely for them to renew the lease.

Also, properties tend to look better in spring. You always want to have units available to show when demand is highest.

An important consideration with these popular move-in dates is where you live. For those close to a college or university, rentals are hot in July and August. You can be sitting on a gold mine if you happen to have apartments in key college towns. But you need to ensure that you have the properties set up to take full advantage. Having rentals in college towns and renewing leases in January can be a big and costly mistake. However, it's important to note that most preferred insurance companies will not allow rentals to college students. Or they will only allow 20-35% of the apartment building to be rented to college students. This is because, historically, college students do not take pride in occupancy. They are hard on the rental and cause more insurance claims than normal.

Other factors can make a difference no matter where you live. One example is tax refunds. So many rely on their tax refund to pay those extra moving charges and this can definitely be factored into your rentals. Be sure to take advantage of that if it would be in an area where this makes a difference. If you have high-end expensive rentals, the tax refunds will more than likely not be a factor.

In Florida, and in many warm-weather states, the "season" (usually October to May) is a great time to have rentals. Snowbirds love the winter months down south and this can be quite profitable. However, many might be looking for shorter term leases, so keep that in mind.

What about short-term rentals? Can you make a profit on renting for shorter periods of time, say three to six months? It depends. In many cases you can make a profit, as some will pay top dollar for short term rentals. However, there can be other factors in play and you will need to decide if having more tenants with shorter terms makes sense to you. For example, can you rent your unit in "season" for higher rates and then during the rest of the year rent it out for smaller periods of time. One thing to consider is that often regulars will come back from out of state and they provide steady income, but that's not always the case. Most insurance policies are more expensive for the "short term" rental.

While we are talking about the best times to rent your properties, also note that there are better times during the year to get great deals on buying rental properties. For example, the winter months might have great deals you can secure. Lower-priced properties and, also, landlords looking to make quick deals are often around during the winter months. This could be a win/win for you and a great way to add more properties to your portfolio!

HERE IS WHAT TO DO NEXT:
- **KNOW AND UNDERSTAND YOUR RENTAL MARKET**
- **IDENTIFY THE DATES THAT DRIVE RENTAL ACTIVITY**
- **CONTACT ME TO DISCUSS YOUR SPECIFIC SITUATION AND GET ANSWERS TO YOUR BURNING QUESTIONS. EMAIL – Russ@InsuranceByCastle.com or PHONE – 800-644-6443 extension 101.**

Chapter 17
Handling Evictions the Right Way

Dealing with evictions is an important part of what you do. Like everything else, it must be handled correctly and legally. You can't lock someone out suddenly, turn off the utilities, or evict tenants without proper notice. Movies and TV shows don't reflect the real story. (Kind-of like those house-flipping shows we talked about earlier.) They, instead, portray an image of an unsuspecting tenant coming home to a notice on their door, the doors locked with their "stuff" outside. This makes for good TV, but is not the way it truly happens. Most states have laws in place prohibiting the landlord from engaging in these types of practices.

Most often, evictions happen for non-payment. Often times, the landlord or property manager has been lenient and worked with the tenant to help. But many times, because of continual non-payment, legal action is required. That is why you want your rental agreements to clearly address payments and policies regarding when rent is due, when payment is considered late, and what, if any, late payment or non-payment penalties there are.

Emergencies can happen. There might be a real reason why a "good tenant" is late or missed payments. Perhaps they lost their job or suffered a medical issue. If this is a good tenant who for years has paid on time, consider the circumstances. However, there may come a point where you have to treat it as a business and make that tough decision to evict. Keep in mind that this is income due you and not having that income can have a negative effect on your business. So, proceed accordingly.

Now, non-payment is not the only reason for eviction. Other reasons include illegal or dangerous activities on a property. A prime example here would be if you discover tenants are selling drugs on your property. It's your responsibility to protect your other tenants, so act quickly.

If the tenant breaks the terms of the lease, then an eviction is also permissible. Say your tenant damages your property and there is the possibility for more damage in the future. You want to act quickly to protect your assets.

Evictions are stressful—not only for the renters, but for the landlords as well. During these times, tension can be felt by all. Renters will often try to fight to stay in a residence and try to challenge the landlord's attempt to evict. The best practice for a landlord is to make sure that they are proceeding in a professional and legal manner. This will help to counteract any potential disagreements during the eviction process.

There are proper steps to take. Property owners and managers must terminate the lease and provide written notice to the renters of the eviction. Laws differ from state to state and what needs to be included in the notice, so it's imperative to check with your local offices to determine that.

The next step is to give the tenants these documents, which then starts the eviction process. By doing so, you are providing written proof of your intent to evict your tenant and the reasons for doing so. Once the process has started, it might be best to stop any additional contact with the tenant. That way the courts can take care of business and, ideally, personal issues won't come into play.

Let's say your tenant does come up with the rent that is due, can you stop the eviction? You can. However, make sure you have payment in full, a good sense that you will receive payments in the future, and determine whether or not you will add on the added expenses you incurred such as court fees, etc. For good tenants, this can prove to be a good business decision.

Once the court approves your eviction, know the tenant's rights. Remember, their rights differ from state to state. Normally, tenants are given a certain amount of time to leave. Once the allotted time period is over, the landlord can then go into the residence and begin the cleanup process. You want to follow the process that is in place for your state.

What happens if your tenants have left furniture or other property that is good? You might have a scenario where renters leave their apartments, but leave all of their belongings behind. In these cases, again abide by your state's rules. Depending on what is left behind makes a difference on how you handle or remove things after a renter has left or been evicted. Trash and garbage are the most common types of things left behind. Usually you are free to dispose of trash. But with their valuables, check your state guidelines and the procedures set in place for these and then proceed according to those guidelines.

Let's say you've done everything right, but you have a tenant that just won't leave. Unfortunately, in cases such as this, law enforcement might need to get involved. Never take matters into your own hands—rather, use the legal means provided you to deal with tenants who aren't complying. The last thing you want is any harm to come to anyone.

Another area you should be aware of is eviction notices without cause. The above examples mainly are for cause (i.e., didn't pay, something went wrong with the tenant, etc.) With eviction notices without cause, the landlord is not required to give a reason. You need to give 30 to 60-day notice (depending on your state). Let's say you decide to sell the premises and, therefore, need the tenants out. This is a prime example of evictions without cause. Just be aware of this and make sure to follow all the rules and regulations of your state. Also, if you are selling your property, find out if the new owners might want to keep the tenants. That's a real possibility and a selling point if you have renters that have been in their apartments for years.

HERE IS WHAT TO DO NEXT:

- **FAMILARIZE YOURSELF WITH YOUR LOCAL EVICTION RULES**
- **KNOW AND UNDERSTAND YOUR EVICTION RESPONSIBILITIES AS A LANDLORD**
- **CREATE AN EVICTION PROCESS**
- **CONTACT ME TO DISCUSS YOUR SPECIFIC SITUATION AND GET ANSWERS TO YOUR BURNING QUESTIONS. EMAIL – <u>Russ@InsuranceByCastle.com</u> or PHONE – 800-644-6443 extension 101.**

Chapter 18
Quick Action for Vacancies - Marketing Your Properties

When you have an apartment turnover in tenants, you need to have a plan for getting the property rented – pronto. Or, better yet, have an established plan to market your properties on an ongoing basis. Think through all the steps needed to get the unit rented. It is not just listing the unit in the various online websites. There is so much more than that to renting. First-time landlords often discover this the hard way.

First, you need to have a list of all the resources available for the listing (online websites, social media, etc.). And, you need to have these even when you have a "full house." Be prepared and don't wait until you have a vacancy to plan ahead.

Set up "templates" or samples of listings so that each time you can do more of a "fill-in-the-blank with information" instead of starting fresh every time. No need to reinvent the wheel. Additionally, routinely review the other listings in your area. That can help you with wording that can appeal to your target tenant best. Of course, we aren't saying copy those listings, but more be aware of specific wording that works and craft your listing with that knowledge.

You need to have the listing worded so that it puts your unit in the best light possible for your target audience. For those family-friendly rentals with young children, emphasize the schools and safety. For any 55 or older listings, discuss safety and outline how close your property is to everything they might need. And of course, for college towns, share why your rental is the one parents will feel best having their kids rent.

Determine the monthly rent, the terms, and any other extras you are including with the rent. In addition, are the utilities included in the rent or are they the responsibility of the tenant? How can the prospective tenant easily contact you? This should all be on the listing.

Bring potential tenants back to your website, so include your web address. Also, on your website you will have more space to go into greater detail than the listing itself so include more detailed information on the property. Consider adding the normal things such as size, number of rooms, rental price, amenities, photos, the eligibility requirements (i.e., credit requirements, pet information, payment procedures, etc.), but also go into greater details on some of the key selling points. If the roof or air conditioner has been recently updated, share it. If you have long-term tenants who rarely move, share it. These extras just might be what get the person to call.

It's good to promote your website as well, because if people don't see it, it does little or no good. Sponsor posts and consider Facebook ads to grow your business page. Social media such as Twitter, Facebook, LinkedIn and Pinterest can be great ways to get your website, and your listings noticed. Always list your units on your business page with details and videos of the unit. People who follow you come to expect this and look forward to these postings, especially if they are looking.

Traditional means of advertising your rental property (such as taking an ad in local newspapers) are still successful. However, many landlords are turning to higher tech ways to get the word out about their available rental properties, using digital marketing.

Start a newsletter on your website so not only can you send out new listings, but you can also provide tips and tricks that will engage your followers. However, if you do a newsletter, commit to sending it out at least once a month. I have found that any less frequently, loses the readers. They come to expect a good newsletter once a month.

Use Rental Websites - One of the most commonly used media forms is the rental website. It is known that millions will search sites like Apartments.com and ApartmentRatings.com to find places to rent, so that can help. Also, do you want to use a site such as Craigslist? Consider the pros and cons of doing so.

Also, don't forget the power of the "For Rent" signs. There are times that this can be enough. On your sign, include a current, valid phone number. Also of importance is making sure that someone will return the calls. Frequently, a potential renter wants to move quickly and, when they don't hear back within a reasonable amount of time, they move on. You can easily lose out on great tenants by just not answering calls promptly.

It's also good to have a "flier box" and keep it full of fliers of the property. Make sure these sell your property well with good wording of the descriptions, etc. Changing a few words can make a big difference. List the price to avoid unnecessary calls and those who can't afford it.

You can also list your rental properties on the MLS. Additionally, many landlords work directly with realtors continuously so they build that relationship.

I know of some landlords that actually have a Referral System. They reward anyone (especially other tenants) if they refer someone to them that ends up renting the property. This can be great marketing. And, the better you are as a landlord, the more your other tenants want to help. Of course, if you make the monetary reward for them a good one that helps too! Word of mouth is so important, so make this work for you.

HERE IS WHAT TO DO NEXT:
- **DRAFT YOUR RENTAL MARKETING STEPS AND PROCESSES**
- **LOOK AT HOW OTHER LANLORDS MARKET THEIR PROPERTIES**
- **USE YOUR WEBSITE AS A DIGITAL MARKETING TOOL TO PROMOTE YOUR PROPERTIES**
- **CONTACT ME TO DISCUSS YOUR SPECIFIC SITUATION AND GET ANSWERS TO YOUR BURNING QUESTIONS. EMAIL – Russ@InsuranceByCastle.com or PHONE – 800-644-6443 extension 101.**

Part 4

Protect Your Property – And ALL Your Assets – From Financial Disaster

Chapter 19
What to Look for in an Insurance Agent & How to Find a Good One

Today, there are so many ways to find an insurance agent. You can call one of the toll-free numbers from TV, go online, ask a friend, etc. It's important to note that finding the right one for your needs is *critical*.

You need to look for the correct people at every step of the process as a landlord. You want to work with the best professionals all along the way. One of your major expenses (in addition to the mortgage, taxes, and maintenance) is insurance. And, don't you want someone on your team who will always be on your side to assist you with any challenges you might have?

Remember that, over the years, you will be forming solid relationships with your insurance agent. They will be the first ones to assist you in your time of need during a claim. It's so much more than just hiring the cheapest or the first one seen online. Unfortunately, many landlords do just that—especially first-time landlords.

Yes, money is important; but it simply cannot be the defining factor. It is smarter to find the right agent—the one that has the most knowledge and can find the best company and protection for each situation. This agent can then offer the best protection for the best prices based on individual needs. So, take the time and do it right.

The agent that has your home and personal auto is not usually knowledgeable in residential rentals, even in the best insurance companies. However, specialists in residential rentals can generally offer good home and personal auto insurance. An insurance specialist might not insure ALL types of residential rentals. So, do your homework and find the best insurance agent in your area or state.

Your insurance agent does not have to be in your area, but the insurance company claims adjustors should be. That is because, nowadays, you deal with an insurance agent more often using email and phone than face-to-face. I insure landlords ALL over California—most of whom I have NEVER met face to face. But the important thing is that my insurance claims adjustors are located all over the state. So, getting claims processed is smooth sailing because they are local to our clients.

I would recommend an independent insurance broker, like myself. We have many different insurance companies with whom we write policies. Because we are not tied to a certain insurance company, we work for the client—in this case, the landlord. We have the landlord's best interest as our first priority and that is truly what you want.

We find the best coverages and premiums for each individual client. In some cases, the client might be best suited to have different insurance policies with different insurance companies. For example, the home and auto insurance might be with insurance Company A. But the landlord insurance policy is with Company B. And the umbrella insurance policy is with Company C. Sounds confusing, but it really isn't. In fact, it is your agent making sure that you are getting the best coverage possible at the best rates and plans for you.

As independent insurance brokers, we represent a large number of clients for any one insurance company. With that volume of policies, we have a certain amount of "clout" with the insurance company. The specialist has even more "clout" due to their knowledge and working relationship with the insurance company.

In addition to getting the best coverages for the client, the premium should be the best as well. If Company A has a large increase in their insurance rates, the independent insurance broker will search the marketplace and make suggestions of other insurance companies that might be better than Company A. This is not available with an insurance agent that represents only one insurance company. Again, an independent agent represents the client to the insurance company. A direct-writing agent is an employee of the insurance company. These direct agents only have one option to offer their clients.

Bottom line is to make sure your insurance professional understands all your needs. Plus, make sure they have experience in insuring the same types of policies that you need. DO NOT think that just because you have your home and auto insurance with Company A, that they will be a good fit for your landlord policy. That is not always the case.

How can you find one? Search Google. Look at their website. Most good agents will have a professional website that shows their expertise. Often, on their site, you will discover that they also blog and write about the very questions you will be asking. That shows they know their stuff, as well. Their website will list the various types of insurance they handle and, of course, this can be key to finding an agent that will have the insurance you need. Simple enough. But also, in reading about the different coverages, does the site explain it well so you can tell they are informed and experienced? Just having the information on their site isn't enough. You also need to feel confident with that information that they are the best at what they do.

Review their social media and start following them. When you start seeing informative tips, you know you are on the right track. Do they respond quickly to posts and are active and engaged? This is another great sign that they will respond quickly to your needs as well.

Talk with friends or others who own investment property. They may have already done a lot of homework and have formed relationships with qualified and trusted agents. See if they have recommendations.

You can look for testimonials on the agent's website and places such as Yelp and social media. Read the testimonials to ensure that they have the experience that you need in the areas you are looking for. A good testimonial from a satisfied client saying that they made the claim's experience less stressful tells you a lot about the agent.

Just to give you some ideas on good testimonials, here are just a few that we have received.

> Exceptional service from a team of seasoned professionals. You will receive nothing but the best from Insurance by Castle. They'll exceed your expectations at every turn!   -- Cathy Mehren Andrew - Facebook

Russ and Ingrid are very knowledgeable. Their fast turn-around makes my job simple - Luis Gregorio

Made finding insurance with a good carrier easy and affordable. Always answer questions and concerns promptly. Getchel Wilson

You answer the phone when calling you. Normally questions are answered while on the 1st call. No need for multiple calls. Paperwork is correct. No errors. – Susan Daniel

Putting all of our properties on one commercial policy reduced our insurance expense by 50 percent, as compared to individual policies for each property through Farmers. – Julie Carson

Again, as we have said throughout, it's so good to have an agent that handles multiple policies – your car, house, apartments, etc. Also, if you happen to have any special needs (say you have high-risk rentals), be open and upfront with your agent so you can discuss your specific requests.

Another place to consider is your state's insurance regulator's website. States have an agency that keeps track of insurance companies, agents, brokers, etc. This can provide the additional information you need.

HERE IS WHAT TO DO NEXT:

- **TALK WITH OTHER INVESTORS ABOUT THE EXPERT TEAM THEY'VE ASSSEMBLED**
- **FIND AN INSURANCE SPECIALIST. FINDING THE RIGHT ONE IS CRITICAL**
- **CONTACT ME TO DISCUSS YOUR SPECIFIC SITUATION AND GET ANSWERS TO YOUR BURNING QUESTIONS. EMAIL – Russ@InsuranceByCastle.com or PHONE – 800-644-6443 extension 101.**

Chapter 20
Why Insurance Specialists are Worth Their Weight in Gold

Insurance Direct Writers (i.e., Farmers, State Farm, Allstate, AAA, etc.) are great insurance companies, but they can only offer insurance through their specific insurance company. This can limit you, the landlord. Additionally, not all insurance companies may offer exactly the types of polices or coverages you may be looking for or need.

A direct writer doesn't have independent representatives write their insurance policies. Normally it is done through their agents, who are their employees, subcontractors, etc. These companies can only write and service insurance for that specific insurance company. For many landlords, that works just fine. These landlords feel they add value doing business with an insurance company they are familiar with (an insurance company whose name they recognize or whose ads they see on TV). However, they may not be experts in the areas of insurance coverage that you may require or they may have a "one-size-fits-all" approach to coverage, which isn't good.

An independent insurance broker has **MANY** companies through which to offer insurance policies. An insurance broker or agent can sell and negotiate insurance for many insurance companies. Since these independent brokers work with several different companies, they can find the best deal with the correct coverage needed for your specific insurance needs.

An independent Insurance niche Specialist, we feel, is the best there is. The specialist knows the industry better than the others. They know which insurance coverages are needed and which ones are not. We have found with residential landlord policies, there are some insurance companies that have coverage added and charged to the customer that are not necessary or needed. Most agents are not aware of these additional costs. This specialist usually knows the various policies inside and out, and will advise accordingly. They know which insurance companies are the best in that particular industry. While many insurance companies are good, they are not all good for all types of policies, niches, or specialties. Some niche specialists even have special EXCLUSIVE programs that **only they** can write for specific insurance companies. This is usually due to the specialist's unique knowledge in that niche. So, do your homework to make the best decisions.

Often, the best price does not always mean the best insurance company or coverage. Try to determine which companies have local claims adjusters in the event that you ever need to make a claim. Finding out how a company handles an insurance claim can make a big difference when the time comes that you really need them.

One thing to note is that no matter which way you go, those licensed have a legal obligation to obtain coverage for you. Rules and regulations are in place that must be followed. These rules are enforced by the State Insurance Department.

As independent insurance agents, we are governed by the California Department of Insurance. This department makes laws on how we can offer proposals to our clients. We are obligated to always offer coverages in the best interest of the client. We, the agents, must look out for the client's interest first and foremost. Because we are independent, we are continually looking for the best rates and coverages for our clients. It is common for us to offer a current client to move from Company A to Company B. This is one of the many advantages of working with an independent agent. We represent the client first.

HERE IS WHAT TO DO NEXT:

- **FIND AN INDEPENDENT INSURANCE NICHE SPECIALIST**
- **CONTACT ME TO DISCUSS YOUR SPECIFIC SITUATION AND GET ANSWERS TO YOUR BURNING QUESTIONS. EMAIL – Russ@InsuranceByCastle.com or PHONE – 800-644-6443 extension 101.**

Chapter 21
Having the Right Insurance Protection –
What You Need to Know to Succeed

Owning residential property is a good investment from the insurance side and, fortunately, insurance rates have never been better for residential rentals. If the rental property does not have much maintenance, then the only other major expenses are taxes and insurance (possibly utilities), and insurance is usually the least of these expenses.

But it's important to have the right coverage and protection because, once you start earning money on your rental investment, an injury or disaster could prove to be a huge financial loss and if you aren't adequately insured, costly problems are sure to arise. We don't want that!

As the landlord, you need to understand coverages and their limits. You have insurance for your peace of mind. If there is a claim, know your coverage and how much the insurance company will pay. I refer to this as the "what lets me sleep at night" type of coverage.

The type of business entity you create also has advantages. For example, being a corporation has its advantages because it protects one's personal assets. However, being a corporation may not cover all assets. For example, it would not cover punitive damages if a tenant is injured or, even worse, killed.

You can see why coverage is so important and why you need to be knowledgeable about it. For example, know that property insurance doesn't necessarily offer enough liability protection. Tenants are extremely important, but so is the actual building that they reside in. If your building is damaged, your primary source of income could be lost. So, property insurance is highly recommended.

Property Insurance Policies have three parts to the coverage, which include:

- The first part is the building amount. This will cover the repair or replacement of the building due to covered losses.
- The second part is the loss of income or the rents that are not being collected while the building is being repaired or rebuilt due to covered losses.
- The third part is the liability coverage for any losses that are proven to be the landlord's fault.

Building coverage will provide monetary compensation in the event that the building is damaged or destroyed. The policy shows the dollar limit the insurance company will pay for these damages. Some insurance companies have endorsements that will offer higher than the limit on the policy. Building code coverage is offered on all preferred insurance policies. It offers extra coverage for "ordinance or law" costs. In most areas of our country, the local city or county has additional ordinances that need to be complied with during the repair or reconstruction of the building. These extra costs are covered with this endorsement up to a certain amount. These expenses can be costly, but your insurance policy may be able to provide considerable financial assistance.

Loss of Income or Loss of Rents. During a covered claim, the insurance policy will cover the loss of rents due to the loss if the tenant is not able to live in the unit or the entire apartment. The landlord still has a mortgage payment and some other expenses. This coverage pays the rent so these expenses can be paid. This is NOT payment for the tenant to rent elsewhere—that is covered under a renter's policy that the tenant can purchase.

Liability Insurance Covers:

- Liability insurance can help pay for damages, medical bills, etc.
- Liability coverage will protect you in the event that someone decides to take legal action against you after experiencing an accident or loss on your property. For example, if a tenant's vehicle is broken into, he or she could potentially file a lawsuit against you. Or if a tenant or guest were to be injured on the premises, they could file a claim accusing the landlord as being the cause of the injury. Most people don't realize that some of the biggest exposure in claims can be legal fees that are necessary in some cases. If your tenants or guests are injured, have adequate coverage
- Umbrella coverage is a more comprehensive form of liability insurance. An umbrella policy offers additional liability limits in addition to the landlord policy. It also can go over the home, autos, and other rentals. In some cases, this can be done all

on the same umbrella policy. Liability and Umbrella coverage are the "peace of mind" coverages. The total limit is up to the client and the amount is again "what lets them sleep at night." There is no correct amount.

Premises Medical Protection provides coverage for medical care in the event that someone is injured while on your property. This is an excellent protective measure for both you and your tenants as it allows your tenants to receive the medical care they need and you are protected against potential lawsuits. This coverage is offered regardless of fault. In most cases, the insurance will pay up to the limit to help reduce potential claims in the future. This is part of the liability portion of the policy.

In addition to the landlord policy, tenants can purchase Renter's Insurance. This policy is purchased by the tenant (not the landlord) and offers the tenant coverage for their belongings, personal liability, and additional rent in the case of a claim. This additional rent is usually when there is a claim on the building and the tenant needs to move to a new or temporary location. This coverage is for the "additional expense" due to this claim. The landlord policy does not offer any coverage for the tenant's belongings or for their rent at another location during the repair or rebuilding of the damaged building.

Whenever possible, have your tenants purchase a Renters' Insurance policy. Not only are they covering their own property and liability, if there is a claim and it is the renter's fault, the landlord (or his/her insurance company) has someone or an insurance company to get repaid by (also known as subrogation). Fortunately, renter's insurance is relatively inexpensive and can cover your tenant and their belongings in the event of a catastrophe such as fire, flood, or theft.

I have two different clients that each had an insurance claim due to a tenant burning a candle that started a fire. Both claims were over $100,000 in damages. Luckily both claims were just property damage and nobody was injured in the fire.

The first client had a tenant that did not have Renter's Insurance. Due to this claim, the insurance rates increased in each of the following three years due to the claim. The insurance policy lost the "loss free credit" even though the claim was not the landlord's fault.

The second client had a tenant that DID have Renter's Insurance. The landlord's insurance company paid the claim. Then that same insurance company was able to get repayment (or subrogation) from the tenant's renter's policy. This client was able to keep his insurance rates low and keep the "loss free credit" on his policy.

The bottom line is that landlords have insurance to help protect their "assets." Try to make sure the tenants do the same.

This leads us to a good point. Can you demand that your tenants have renter's insurance? Yes and no! You need to be aware of the laws in your area. In some areas, you are allowed to require Renter's Insurance to all tenants and, in other areas, it is against the law to require this insurance. This is something you may want to check in your area and, of course, if it is allowed, make it a requirement.

Here is some good news. Insurance on rental properties is a tax deduction. These deductions include the premiums you pay for all types of rentals including insurance. Even landlord liability insurance can be deducted.

There are other considerations as well. For example, you'll need to obtain insurance specifically for rental properties, even if you are renting out your own home. Standard homeowner's insurance policies will not offer protection if you rent your home and haven't informed your insurance company.

There are many differences with a home policy and a rental policy. Here are a few:

- The liability insurance is different for owner-occupied homes versus a rental property (as a landlord).
- Most home policies can cover rental at a temporary site when a claim makes the owner move out of the home during the covered claim. A rental policy covers the loss of rents for this exposure (not the tenant's rent at a temporary location).
- A rental policy premium for a home is lower than if it were a homeowner's policy. This is because the personal property limit is lower and the liability is not as broad when only for a rental home.

- There is usually a small amount, if any, of insurance for contents or property at the location for a rental property.

In addition to the above, here are some additional tips:

- Know your policy and coverage. Take the time to read and evaluate everything. Don't assume anything when it comes to coverage. Know what is covered and what is not in case of accident or damage to the property. If in doubt, ask your agent. In most cases, it is better to have one agent handle all your policies. They will know you and your business best and be sure you are covered in all areas.
- Pay attention to the exceptions. Just as important as what is covered, is what isn't covered. Know what isn't covered and also know if some things have a higher deductible.
- Re-evaluate your insurance needs with your insurance agent every two or three years. Changes in property and policies can potentially save a great deal of money. Consider bundling policies if you have several properties.
- Always keep your important documentation safe and secure. Knowing where your important information is located is important and also having it safe in case of any disaster; will prevent challenges down the road.
- Most insurance companies offer a better rate if the landlord has multiple locations on the same policy. It is called a "multiple building discount." The

insurance companies feel that, for most claims such as a small fire, the likelihood that more than one building being damaged is small.

As you can see, there is a lot to consider regarding property and insurance to keep your property investments safe and secure.

HERE IS WHAT TO DO NEXT:

- **START REVIEWING AND EVALUATING THE DIFFERENT COVERAGES AND PROTECTIONS**
- **REVIEW PROPERTY INSURANCE POLICIES**
- **REVIEW BUILDING COVERAGES**
- **REVIEW LIABILITIY COVERAGES**
- **REVIEW UMBRELLA POLICES**
- **KNOW YOUR POLICIES AND COVERAGES. TAKE THE TIME TO READ AND EVALUATE EVERYTHING.**
- **CONTACT ME TO DISCUSS YOUR SPECIFIC SITUATION AND GET ANSWERS TO YOUR BURNING QUESTIONS. EMAIL – Russ@InsuranceByCastle.com or PHONE – 800-644-6443 extension 101.**

Chapter 22
Smart Investors Build an Expert Team

With a "Niche Specialist" as your insurance agent, you know you have an agent that knows their niche better than all others. From an insurance perspective, niche specialists know the coverages and are better at understanding the needs and requirements of their clients.

Some niche specialists have an "exclusive program." This is usually exclusive to just that agent and that agent is the only one that can offer this "special program." This comes from years of experience in that niche and offering insurance coverages that are exclusive to just that agent.

For example, I have an exclusive "7 Doors or More" ™ program. This is exclusive to just my agency. This allows the rental owner of multiple single-family rentals to combine all these locations onto one policy. This can be all rental homes or a combination of homes, duplexes, triplexes, etc. As long as there are seven units or more owned by the same entity, they can be insured on one policy. This gets the best rate, the best discount, and fewer hassles of multiple policies. In addition, this program has better coverage.

Having an exclusive program shows the rental owner that the insurance agent is a step above the "normal" agent. They have a specialty that also benefits the rental owner.

In some cases, the Niche Specialist is also in that niche, which is an even greater benefit. In my case, I am also a landlord and understand firsthand the ups and down of all insurance coverage. This gives me further insight into the specific needs and coverage for this type of program and allows me to tailor the coverage based on first-hand experience. I am able to look at both sides of the insurance policy. I am "one of you", my fellow landlords.

Also, often times those who are "niche specialists" also engage team members who also help in this area. They know the ropes of the business well and their clients' unique needs through dealing with the clients regularly, and they can best offer help in those areas.

In our agency, we insure thousands of landlords all over California. Our exclusive "7 Doors or More" ™, has the best rates available. Most of our owners are just as happy because they now can have all their locations on one policy. This helps eliminate getting multiple bills and policies, and the overall headache of keeping track of all these policies. These specialists have the client in mind and offer more than just price. In our agency, we want to offer the best "ease of use" with all our clients and their insurance program.

HERE IS WHAT TO DO NEXT:

- **REVIEW YOUR NICHE SPECIALIST EXCLUSIVE PROGRAMS**
- **CHECK OUT OUR EXCLUSIVE 7-DOOR PROGRAM, IT IS ONE OF THE BEST AROUND**
- **CONTACT ME TO DISCUSS YOUR SPECIFIC SITUATION AND GET ANSWERS TO YOUR BURNING QUESTIONS. EMAIL – <u>Russ@InsuranceByCastle.com</u> or PHONE – 800-644-6443 extension 101.**

Chapter 23
Secrets to Saving Money
on Your Real Estate Premiums

Insurance is one of the necessities of owning rental properties and one of the larger expenses, other than mortgages and taxes. It is an absolute must to have and it is extremely important to fully understand your coverage for each property you own. This is especially beneficial if you own multiple properties.

It's good to work with an agent you trust who can walk you through all that is required and not only will ensure you are protected, but save you money as well. Our clients love the fact that we are always looking out for them in coverage as well as savings.

Fortunately, there are ways to save on premiums. Here are a few tips:

- Keep the number of claims to a minimum. Your policy gives you a discount for being "claims free." This discount can be as much as 20-25%. Insurance is in place for those major claims, but not necessarily for the smaller ones. If the claim is double the deductible or more, then it is worth submitting to the insurance company.
- Review your deductible and the options for lowering or raising the deductible. You will be surprised how much, or even how little, the premium difference is as you go up or down. Make informed decisions based not only on the

property, but your financial outlook as well. Ask your agent the premium for various deductibles and then decide once you have all the facts. Take into consideration that if a claim were to occur, would you have the deductible on hand to pay for it or a means to get this money? It might sound good on paper to have a high deductible and lower initial costs, but if a claim occurs and you can't get the money together for the deductible, it can backfire.

- Most insurance companies offer discounts for bundling all of your insurance policies with them. Shop around for the best deals on bundles and you're likely to save. Most companies will give discounts for bundling your home insurance and your automobile insurance. But some will also provide discounts for other types of policies as well. It pays to call and find out.
- Make sure you understand what coverages are needed and what coverages are not for your particular building. That way you don't pay for extras you don't need. These should be reviewed frequently, too.
- If you have multiple buildings on one policy, look to see if they can "blanket" the building limit for no extra charge. "Blanketing" means adding all the building limits on one policy with the insurance company using up to that total amount available for one claim. This is extremely important when you need to rebuild. In some cases, there is NO EXTRA charge for this endorsement.

- Know what is the lowest replacement cost per foot for the buildings? If you are "blanketing," the insurance company will provide a minimum cost per square foot. But if at the time of the claim it costs more than expected, which often happens, the limits from the other locations are available for that claim. You can see how beneficial that would be if a claim were to be substantial.
- You should review your insurance every two to three years or so.

Work closely with your agent and develop a relationship. By developing that closeness, the agent is more aware of your needs and will be able to best keep you informed. Also try to have your agent handle all your insurance needs so that he can help prevent any "gaps" in coverage that you might not be aware of.

HERE IS WHAT TO DO NEXT:

- **REVIEW YOUR DEDUCTIBLE AND THE OPTIONS FOR LOWERING OR RAISING THE DEDUCTIBLE**
- **SHOP AROUND FOR THE BEST DEALS ON INSURANCE BUNDLES**
- **PLAN ON AND SCHEDULE INSURANCE REVIEWS EVERY TWO TO THREE YEARS OR SO**
- **CONTACT ME TO DISCUSS YOUR SPECIFIC SITUATION AND GET ANSWERS TO YOUR BURNING QUESTIONS. EMAIL – Russ@InsuranceByCastle.com or PHONE – 800-644-6443 extension 101.**

Chapter 24
Landlord Insurance – Why is it needed

It's important to know that as a landlord and property owner, you often face unexpected surprises and issues that pop-up with your residential rental properties. While landlord insurance is not required, it's a wise choice to have if you regularly rent out your property (and don't live on the premises). Landlord insurance is designed to protect you from loss of rental income as a result of damage to your rental unit from fire, inclement weather conditions, and other uncontrollable factors that might leave your unit vacant until damages are fixed.

If there is a mortgage on the rental, the lender will REQUIRE a landlord insurance policy for full replacement of the building (or the loan value). This policy will cover the building, the loss of rents, and liability insurance in the case of an injury.

Did you know that if you file a claim on a rental property, but the policy is not considered a Landlord Policy, the insurance company may reject the claim? Not good. Not good at all!

It's important to know that not all landlord insurance policies are created the same; some policies may include one or all of the following types of damage. The basic components of a landlord insurance policy include:

- **Property damage:** covers damage to your property from fire, theft, inclement weather, etc.

- **Liability insurance:** covers any liability lawsuits and claims from visitors or tenants.
- **Loss of income:** covers loss of rent in case your property is uninhabitable.

The Various Types of Landlord Insurance Categories include:

"DP" stands for dwelling policy:

DP-1: This is a very basic policy that just covers common incidents such as fire and vandalism.

Make sure you do not have this type of policy.

DP-2: A more comprehensive policy that covers less common incidents including damage from storms and if a car damages your building. Make sure you do not have this type of policy. It is VERY restrictive. Make sure you only get this type of policy as a last resort.

DP-3: The most comprehensive policy that essentially covers all potential perils; however, it may have some exclusions. This is the most common type of policy for rental houses, duplexes, triplexes and fourplexes.

Commercial package policies (called CPP) or Commercial Business Owners Policies (called BOPs)

This is a commercial policy and the BEST available for apartment buildings (5 units and higher). If you can get this type of policy for your smaller residential rental, it is advisable. The coverages and limits are usually higher with the premium being the same or better than the DP policies.

These policies may reimburse you via cash value, OR replacement value of damaged items (often a more accurate reflection and higher amount).

Important Clauses to Keep in Mind include:

Replacement Cost for Building Coverage:Shop around for an insurance policy that includes Replacement Cost for Building Coverage. Building coverage includes basic structural damage to your property including plumbing, piping, fixtures and any fixed appliances. Replacement cost provides you with the money to replace your building at the time of the incident, rather than the replacement cost at the time you took out your policy. In years past the term has been "guaranteed" replacement cost, but in most cases today, the "guaranteed" has been removed. This is due to some court cases that the old building had older wood (i.e. 75- to 100-year-old redwood). The rebuilding could not "guarantee" the same older wood. So, the new endorsement is for "like and similar" construction. In older buildings, the walls could have lathe and plaster walls. The replacement would be sheetrock.

Flood Damage: This is a separate type of policy. It's never a good day if your property is damaged via a burst pipe. Plumbing issues are generally covered with a basic policy, however, consider getting water and flood damage, which covers natural disasters and unforeseen sewer backups. In areas that are in a flood plain, the lenders will require this additional policy.

Acts of Nature: If you live in an area that is prone to hurricanes, tornados, and earthquakes, consider getting insurance coverage for acts of nature. This coverage is something that needs to be specifically requested.

Fair Rental Income Protection: Should your property become uninhabitable due to some type of damage, this policy can provide you with fair rent for a specified amount of time. Note that this doesn't cover vacancies or loss of rent from tenants who don't pay. In most DP or Commercial Policies, they offer 12 months of loss of rents due to a "covered" claim. So, if there is a fire and the tenant is not able to live in the unit, the landlord will receive the rent (or up to the limit on the policy) for as many as 12 months; or as long as the repairs take to make the building habitable again. Once the repairs are complete, this loss of rent stops.

Having a strong landlord insurance policy can get you out of a financial pinch should you need help. Do your research about different policies and never assume your policy provides certain types of coverage without full knowledge that it does.

HERE IS WHAT TO DO NEXT:
- **FIND A GOOD LANDLORD POLICY**
- **LEARN THE DIFFERENCES BETWEEN DP1, DP2, AND DP3**
- **CONTACT ME TO DISCUSS YOUR SPECIFIC SITUATION AND GET ANSWERS TO YOUR BURNING QUESTIONS. EMAIL – Russ@InsuranceByCastle.com or PHONE – 800-644-6443 extension 101.**

Chapter 25
Ins & Outs of Umbrella Liability Insurance

An umbrella liability insurance policy offers additional liability insurance over the underlying policies. Liability insurance is designed to help protect you from major lawsuits, claims, and more. So, when a landlord has a claim, the landlord's insurance policy will pay up to the limit of liability. In addition, the liability portion of the policy will pay for the legal fees to defend the claim. In most cases, this is the most important part of the liability coverage.

In some cases, the landlord's policy does not offer enough coverage for the claim or exposure. That is where an umbrella policy comes into play. An umbrella policy is written in limits of millions (i.e., $1 million, $2 million, and more). Most landlords have an umbrella policy to protect their assets, financial well-being, etc. A PERSONAL liability policy can cover the normal limits of a homeowner's policy, auto policy, some rental policies, boats, RVs, and others.

When you consider that one claim could substantially wipe you out, you can see the benefit to having this added protection. For many who have worked hard their entire life, an umbrella policy offers the added protection to make sure they are protected beyond the normal coverage. And best yet, it is usually very affordable.

So how it works: when an insured has a claim against them, their primary insurance policies pay up to their limits, and then any additional amount will be handled by their umbrella policy, up to the limits of that policy. Awesome—right?

Here's a prime example. We had a client that had an apartment building that was two stories. The tenant had a visitor that was walking down the outside stairs and the heel of the man's shoe caught on a step. He not only fell, but the heel was caught on the step. After the investigation, it was determined this was the landlord's fault. The insurance policy for the apartment building had a limit of $1,000,000 per occurrence (or per claim). However, the injuries, medical bills (including multiple surgeries), loss of wages, etc., totaled $1,560,000. The apartment policy paid the limit of that policy or $1,000,000. The client would have been on the hook for the balance or $560,000. Fortunately, we had this client purchase an umbrella policy and he chose the $1,000,000 limit. So, the personal umbrella paid the balance of $560,000. The claim was paid in full by the insurance policies. You can just imagine the relief this landlord experienced by having made the right choice in insurance coverage!

This personal umbrella policy covered all of our client's cars, home, and apartment for under $750 per year. Cheap versus the $560,000 he would have had to pay out of his pocket. We try to ALWAYS offer our landlords a personal umbrella proposal with various limits available. Once you know the premium, you decide what the best solution is for you. We are so glad our client knew these options prior to the claim, versus saying "If I knew, I would have purchased it."

A couple things you should know about these policies:

- Often times those with higher assets want umbrella insurance coverage, but everyone should look at this coverage, even a renter or at least those that own a home. This isn't only for those higher income families or businesses.

- Umbrella policies only cover those policies that are listed. You are not automatically covered unless the insurance company has the vehicles, home, rentals, etc., listed on that policy. So just because you have an umbrella coverage on your home, don't think it will automatically cover your car. This is something to be discussed with your agent, who will look out for your best interest.

- Not all umbrella policies can cover all these items. Some personal umbrella policies will only cover your vehicles and home. Then you need to purchase a commercial umbrella for the rentals. Again, this discussion is best made between you and your insurance agent.

- While most personal umbrella policies go over personal polices and commercial umbrellas go over commercial polices, there are some personal umbrella policies with various companies that will go over personal policies and some commercial policies (usually landlords only). It will save on the total premium if you can get a personal umbrella to go over these policies. First of all, the premiums are usually much more affordable and having one umbrella policy is so much easier.

HERE IS WHAT TO DO NEXT:

- **GET AN UMBRELLA POLICY**
- **CONTACT ME TO DISCUSS YOUR SPECIFIC SITUATION AND GET ANSWERS TO YOUR BURNING QUESTIONS. EMAIL – Russ@InsuranceByCastle.com or PHONE – 800-644-6443 extension 101.**

Chapter 26
The Inside Scoop on Admitted & Non-Admitted Insurance Companies

There's a difference between admitted insurance companies and non-admitted insurance companies. According to an article on Clarkeandsampson.com, an admitted carrier is defined as, "One that follows guidelines set forth by the state, and is therefore, licensed in the state or country in which the insured's exposure is located. Of course, these guidelines vary from state to state, and some are more stringent than others. The obligation to follow state regulations and submit rates to a state's department of insurance limits the flexibility of the insurer. If an admitted carrier becomes insolvent, the state guaranty fund steps in to pay out claims and premium remuneration where applicable."

This fund is available for policyholders when an admitted company is not able to meet all the financial claim's requirements. Usually what has happened is the admitted insurance company has gone out of business. This fund is not a guarantee of payment, but a way to get some of the money that is due them. If the policyholder is with a NON-ADMITTED company, it is between the policyholder and the insurance company. In other words, it is you against the insurance company and you can see where problems might start.

An article on Insurancethoughtleadership.com best defines non-admitted insurance carriers as,

"An excess and surplus line carrier and operates in a state without going through the approval process required for admitted companies. Non-admitted carriers are not bound by filed forms or rates and therefore have much greater flexibility to write and design policies to cover unique and specific risks, and to adjust premiums accordingly. When standard markets can't or won't write a risk, or when an admitted carrier cannot offer the appropriate terms, the non-admitted market is available to fill this gap. Non-admitted insurance carriers are regulated by the state Surplus Lines offices, but regulation is far less invasive than for the admitted markets. The most obvious difference between admitted and non-admitted is that purchasers of non-admitted policies do NOT have the protection afforded by the state's guaranty fund."

When it comes to residential rentals in California, you want to, when possible, get insurance with an admitted insurance company. You also want to look at the rating of the insurance company. If possible ALWAYS use an "A" rated company. Do the research on your carrier to ensure that they are admitted in your state.

Just being non-admitted doesn't necessarily mean they aren't regulated.

At Insurance by Castle, we always use admitted companies when available. The amount of business we have with non-admitted insurance companies is less than 2% of our policies. When it comes to residential landlord policies in California, I would say we don't have ANY non-admitted companies. The only exception would be for a landlord that has a building that is in an area that the admitted companies will not insure.

HERE IS WHAT TO DO NEXT:

- **FAMILARIZE YOURSELF WITH THE ADMITTED VS NON-ADMITTED CARRIERS**
- **FAMILARIZE YOURSELF WITH THE RATINGS OF THE ADMITTED VS NON-ADMITTED CARRIERS**
- **CHOOSE AN ADMITTED CARRIER TO WORK WITH**
- **CONTACT ME TO DISCUSS YOUR SPECIFIC SITUATION AND GET ANSWERS TO YOUR BURNING QUESTIONS. EMAIL – Russ@InsuranceByCastle.com or PHONE – 800-644-6443 extension 101.**

Chapter 27
What is a BOP or CPP and Why You Need to Know

BOP is an insurance term meaning "Business Owners Policy." This is a "packaged" policy meaning it has all the main coverage you would need for a residential rental policy—Building Coverage, Loss of Rents, and Liability. In addition to basic protection, most insurance companies have added extra coverage that will provide the best protection for that type of policy. For example: Ordinance or Law Coverage, Backup of Sewage, Replacement Cost on buildings, etc.

Many apartment policies are written with BOP policies. BOP policies are written on mostly the apartments from 5-50 units. However, in some cases, if the apartment complex has multiple buildings, a BOP policy could be used for more than 50 units.

CPP is an insurance term meaning "Commercial Package Policy." This policy is specified by the agent regarding what coverages are needed and can be more custom-made. The insurance company's underwriter will review and make any adjustments that they see fit. There are many parts to this type of policy (i.e., the building coverage, the liability coverage, the loss of rents, etc.). In residential landlord policies, this type of policy is usually only used for larger complexes. One reason being larger complexes usually have a business office. This type of policy would offer the coverage needed for these types of exposure.

Early on in my career, I did not understand the difference in these two types of policies. I had a client for whom I was shopping all my insurance companies for his apartment building. With the first company, I rated the apartment building in a "BOP" policy and the premium was $2600. In the next company, they did not offer BOP policies, so I rated the apartment in a CPP policy. In the CPP policy, I had to add each coverage I wanted on the policy and the premium came to $3400 (plus some coverage that was not available on this CPP). From that point on, for apartment complexes that were up to 50 units, I always used the BOP. Therefore, in the larger complexes you need to look at both BOPs and CPPs

For example, if you are a landlord for a complex under 50 units, you will usually have a BOP policy. This policy will cover all the areas needed. In addition, it will have "extras" at no additional premium. These "extras" are designed for the landlord policy.

If your building has over 50 units you will most likely be on a CPP policy. This type of policy has "added" these extras to cover all exposures in that complex. In some cases, you could be insured on a BOP. You should confirm what you have and discuss the pros and cons with your agent.

Owners of BOPS often find benefit in how easy it is compared to other policies. For first-time investors, that can prove beneficial.

In residential landlord policies, there are three primary coverage options:

1. Building – Damage or total loss to the structure
2. Loss of Rents – When the building is damaged or destroyed, the tenant is not paying rent. The insurance will pay the lost rents to the landlord for a certain period of time. The tenant will not be paid under this coverage.
3. Liability – This is coverage if the landlord is liable for damages done to someone (usually medical in nature). As important, this coverage also pays for the defense of claims. If the BOP or CPP limit is not enough, then you can purchase an umbrella policy to increase the total liability protection. When the BOP or CPP policy limit is used up, then the umbrella picks up after that to the limit of the umbrella policy.

A good thing to note as well is worker's compensation coverage would not be included in either of these policies and a separate policy would be required for that. You would need this type of insurance policy if you have any employees working for you (i.e. on-site managers).

HERE IS WHAT TO DO NEXT:

- **LEARN THE DIFFERENCES BETWEEN CPP'S AND BOP'S**
- **CONTACT ME TO DISCUSS YOUR SPECIFIC SITUATION AND GET ANSWERS TO YOUR BURNING QUESTIONS. EMAIL – Russ@InsuranceByCastle.com or PHONE – 800-644-6443 extension 101.**

Chapter 28
How "Blanketing" Can Keep You Out of Trouble

In insurance terms, "Blanketing the Buildings" means where there are multiple locations on a policy, the insurance company will add all the building limits and use the total of the building limits for any one claim. Some companies will do this for no extra premium. The insurance company would still require each building to be insured to the correct and true replacement amount. It can apply to one location with multiple properties or properties at different locations.

This differs from "Specified Limit," which is a specific limit set on a property. With this coverage, the most the insurance company will pay is that specific limit that was set up.

Here's what you need to look for in these types of policies:

- If you choose specified limit, make sure what you have covered is enough. Review when you make improvements, your property increases in value, etc. You need that added protection to cover that specific amount.
- For blanket limits, the advantage is the entire limit is available for losses.
- Coverage for blanket limits can add to the premium. Review with your agent to make sure it's the best coverage for you and the pros and cons for your business.

- Be mindful of margin clauses. Some will add this to policies as an endorsement and it can reduce what you will receive from a loss. We feel it is not needed, so check with your agent and if you find that it is on your policy, have your agent let you know if you should remove it or not.

I had a client with a "blanket limit" for all five of his apartments located all over California. He insured all locations on one policy. He had a claim at one location and the limit was what the client and insurance company thought was correct. However, at the time of the claim, there was an unusual shortage of some of the material needed and, thus, the cost per square foot was higher than expected. Thanks to the "blanket limit" on this policy, the claim was paid in full with no issues. The total amount of the building coverage on the claim was $675,000. The claim was $722,000. However, the total of all five apartments was $3,256,000. This coverage was at no EXTRA CHARGE for this policy. This is another reason having the right insurance agent is key to your success. They insure you are covered so you can sit back, relax, and take care of business.

It should be noted that deductibles will apply for both types of coverage.

<u>HERE IS WHAT TO DO NEXT:</u>

- **UNDERSTAND BLANKETING AND DECIDE IF YOU NEED ONE**
- **CONTACT ME TO DISCUSS YOUR SPECIFIC SITUATION AND GET ANSWERS TO YOUR BURNING QUESTIONS. EMAIL – <u>Russ@InsuranceByCastle.com</u> or PHONE – 800-644-6443 extension 101.**

Chapter 29
Vacant vs Occupied & Your Liability

If your home or property is empty for 60 days or more, it may be considered "vacant" or "unoccupied." That makes a big difference in your insurance and it's important to understand the differences because, for insurance companies, there is a difference between vacant and unoccupied as far as claims are concerned. Typically, insurance for unoccupied properties tend to be less than what is required for vacant properties. So, let's break it down.

The time when one tenant moves out and the next tenant moves in is usually referred to as "unoccupied." But not all insurance companies define when "unoccupied" becomes vacant. In most cases, the first 20-60 days can be considered "unoccupied." And then over 60 days, the unit becomes vacant. Once the location has a vacant unit, the insurance coverages are greatly reduced, which in turn, means more liability to you. Often times, not everything is covered that would be covered if the unit was not vacant.

If a rental unit is not occupied or is vacant, a claim can become substantially higher. To see why, here is just one prime example. Say the water connection to a toilet was to start leaking—the tenant would notice this very soon after the leak starts. If the rental unit was not occupied or vacant, the damages become exponentially larger as there is no one there to notice and, thus, respond quickly. You also find more problems with apartments being vandalized and burglarized because no one is on the premises.

We have had more than one claim that would have been minor if the unit had a tenant. And, unfortunately, because no one was around, the damage increased and led to thousands of dollars in claims. A small leak that goes undetected soon becomes very extensive because it continues. This is especially true if the leak is on the second or third floor. The damage spreads to the lower floors. And as you can imagine, multiple units can be affected.

This is something the insurance company does not want to happen and that is why the preferred insurance companies will not insure if they know the rental is VACANT. Or, if there is a large percentage of an apartment building that is vacant, they are more inclined not to insure.

It should also be noted that coverage for a vacant home or other property may be more restrictive than regular home and landlord insurance. Therefore, it might not cover everything you would expect it to.

NOTE: Most preferred insurance companies that cover apartment buildings have a threshold of no more than 20-35% unoccupied at any time. The insurance companies know that in an apartment building there could be a small percentage in transition at any given time. Bottom line—get a tenant as soon as possible.

There are also other considerations that most don't think of as well. Say you leave your home for several weeks; it can void your homeowner's insurance policy in some cases, but not all. Once again, the risk of theft, water damage, fire and more is greater if no one is home. The solution—if you plan on leaving for an extended period of time, contact your insurance agent. This one call can save you considerable money down the road by just knowing what is covered and if they need to add in an endorsement or something similar to keep you covered.

Also, what about those who have a summer home and a winter residence? Check with your agent to determine the best plan there. Check with both state's requirements if your homes are in different states, which often times they are. The requirements might differ so it's best to be informed.

One thing to note, don't try and hide the fact that your home is vacant or unoccupied. Many think "they'll never know," which is not entirely true. It's pretty easy to tell if a residence has been left unattended. A claim can be denied based on this, so always be upfront and honest.

If you routinely divide your time between a primary home and a vacation home, you may choose to purchase a package covering both properties when you are and are not in residence.

HERE IS WHAT TO DO NEXT:
- **UNDERSTAND THE DIFFERENCE BETWEEN VACANT AND UNOCCUPIED**
- **CONTACT ME TO DISCUSS YOUR SPECIFIC SITUATION AND GET ANSWERS TO YOUR BURNING QUESTIONS. EMAIL – Russ@InsuranceByCastle.com or PHONE – 800-644-6443 extension 101.**

Chapter 30
Tips for Insuring Multiple Locations

When owning multiple units, there is a good rule of thumb—for every ten units or so, you should make a separate LLC.

For example, if you own 18 rental homes, then have one LLC for the first ten and a second LLC for the remaining eight. Or, if you own two apartment complexes, one with 18 units and a second with eight units; take title to each apartment in separate LLCs. The main reason for this is to protect your assets.

In the event of a large claim against the owner, the courts could look to the rental income as a way to pay the claim. If all the rentals are in one LLC, then all the rental income could be subject to a judgement against the LLC. If the LLC only has ten units or so, then the courts can only look at those ten units.

I had a client with a substantial liability claim against them and the courts only looked at the assets in that one LLC. This one LLC was only nine units. The owner had a total of 49 units. These properties were held in title in multiple LLCs. This protected the other assets from this particular judgment. You can imagine what a difference that makes!

Now let's discuss different types of business entities. In your business, one of the important considerations you have to make is how you are going to protect all your assets the best way possible. One way to do that is through the type of business you form. It's sad to say, but being the owner of apartment units can often make you a target. In today's lawsuit-friendly environment, where people sue for almost any reason, you need that added protection. Say you have a slip and fall, tenants can and will look for not only reimbursement for their medical bills, but also other damages such as pain and suffering, loss of wages, etc. You don't always want to constantly be worried about these consequences.

Of course, we encourage you to consult with your legal advisor for information in your particular area, but knowing this can be instrumental in your asset protection.

And speaking of protecting your assets, we also encourage you to look into umbrella policies (see Chapter 16 on Umbrella Policies for additional information).

So what exactly is an LLC? LLCs are the most popular way to take title these days. It is a separate entity from your personal assets and, therefore, adds another layer of protection. If a property is owned by an individual in their name only, then the owner's personal assets can be at risk. This can lead to someone losing virtually all of their personal assets. If a claim is brought against someone who has formed an LLC, only the LLC's assets are at risk. You can imagine how important that can be, especially if you own multiple locations.

For tax purposes, forming an LLC eliminates the "double taxation." The income is claimed on the owner's individual tax return. LLCs with only one owner are taxed as a sole proprietorship with no additional taxes.

It's also very important to meet with your accountant or tax advisor and find out exactly what can be written off – and keep thorough records of all deductions.

One disadvantage of an LLC is that they can have recurring yearly fees and these fees can be pricey. But we believe the advantages outweigh the added costs and that having that piece of mind to protect your assets is worth it.

Another disadvantage is that some lenders are hesitant to loan money to an LLC. Many can, however, get loans with their personal backing. Again, something you want to consider.

You should also familiarize yourself with the different types of businesses you can form (i.e., C or S corporations, partnerships, trusts, etc.) Determine what is best for you.

Being a landlord has its ups and downs for sure; however, when you do more of the right things while getting set up and maintaining your properties, you'll have less stress and fewer negatives that happen in the day-to-day operations of your business. That is priceless!

HERE IS WHAT TO DO NEXT:

- SEEK PROFESSIONAL TAX ADVICE
- FIND A GREAT ATTORNEY TO ADD TO YOUR TEAM OF EXPERTS
- SETUP YOUR INVESTMENT THROUGH AN LLC OR THE ADVICE PROVIDED BY YOUR CPA AND ATTORNEY
- CONTACT ME TO DISCUSS YOUR SPECIFIC SITUATION AND GET ANSWERS TO YOUR BURNING QUESTIONS. EMAIL – Russ@InsuranceByCastle.com or PHONE – 800-644-6443 extension 101.

Chapter 31
The Insurance Claims Process &
What You Need to Know

Let's face it– having a claim against your property is no fun and can add additional stress. But being prepared and having everything in order right from the beginning will help enormously.

When you have a claim on a residential rental there are a few items that you need to make sure of. These include:

- When the claim happens, take all steps necessary to ensure all parties are safe. If medical attention is needed, do not delay—call 911. If there is property damage, do all you can to help keep the damage as minimal as possible. Be quick to make the right decisions based on the gravity of the situation.
- Safety is always the top priority. Your safety, your tenant' safety, and even the public's safety. Take immediate action as appropriate.
- Once the claim happens, make sure no more damage is caused. This includes, if necessary, securing or boarding off the area so no one else can get injured. It's more than just making sure everyone stays clear of the area. Often the professionals take over and will assist. Let them do their jobs!
- The main thing you want to do is gather enough information to be able to contact your insurance company to file a claim.

- DOCUMENT all the details and take pictures. You want to gather enough information to be able to assist your insurance company in filing a claim. This is the key for the claim process to be successful. Police reports, pictures, statements from tenants, and anything else related to the incident or problem should be organized and kept.
- Once you are able, contact your insurance agent to advise him or her of the claim. In most cases they will talk you through the process and confirm if the claim is worth submitting. Complete all paperwork quickly to ensure resolution of your claim as quickly as possible.
- Your claims adjustor will advise you further of the steps involved in moving forward. Tell them all the circumstances you know about the claim and all parties involved. Do not lie or conceal any facts. If you do, there could be issues with the settlement of the claim.
- Once the claim is in process, the insurance company will pay the company that is doing the repairs directly (less your deductible) in most cases. Track the progress and payments if possible.
- NOTE: You want to make sure the limits are enough to cover the claim, but NOT over-insured, as the overage will not be paid if the claim can be fixed for a lower amount. Consult your insurance agent for more information to make sure you have the correct limits and coverages.
- Once the claim is complete, it will be closed by the insurance company and they should have you sign off to confirm all items are repaired or replaced.

Make sure you are satisfied that the claim is completely done before signing anything.

- For a total of three to five years after the claim, your insurance policy will lose the "loss free" credit due to this claim. In some cases, if the claim is small enough or if the insurance company is able to subrogate against the party that caused the damage and recover the costs of the claim, then the "loss free credit" will continue.

NOTE: This is why it is VERY helpful if your tenants have renter's insurance. If they cause the claim, the landlord's insurance company has another insurance company to repay them.

COMMENT: A good rule of thumb on claims, if the claim is less than double to triple the deductible, DO NOT turn it in. Your premiums will increase over the next 3 plus years more than amount of the claim. Talk to your agent if there are any questions.

HERE IS WHAT TO DO NEXT:
- **DRAFT A CLAIMS CHECK LIST**
- **CONTACT ME TO DISCUSS YOUR SPECIFIC SITUATION AND GET ANSWERS TO YOUR BURNING QUESTIONS. EMAIL – <u>Russ@InsuranceByCastle.com</u> or PHONE – 800-644-6443 extension 101.**

Chapter 32
One Size Does Not Fit All

When it comes to owning, as well as insuring, residential rentals, ONE SIZE DOES NOT FIT ALL.

What do we mean by that? You, as the residential landlord, need to do your homework and find out what you want. Do you want single family rentals, small rentals buildings (3-4 units) or apartment building of medium or larger sizes? Do you want to self-manage or hire a management company for some or all tasks?

Do you already know or have the skills of managing properties and all of the work it can entail? Are you willing to learn the ropes, often at some expense? There are many different responsibilities in property ownership and rentals, from purchasing and planning, repairs and upkeep, money collection and possible eviction, just to name a few.

While going at it on your own can sometimes seem like a daunting process, it can be done and done quite profitably, even for those just starting out. But know, too, that oftentimes you can form alliances with others who have the business or real estate expertise you may not have. For example, you can form alliances with those in construction or those with handyman expertise, etc. Just remember to go with someone you truly trust as often problems surface when things go wrong.

Property management companies can assist in either some or all of the details of rental management.

Management companies charge different rates and fees depending on numerous things including the area, property, number of units, work required, etc. Usually there is an initial placement fee and yearly renewal fees that are often based upon the total rental amounts. An owner must be careful that any or all profit is not eaten up in the fees and expenses of the property management company.

With regards to insurance agents, the same is true—not all insurance agents are the same. If possible, you want a specialist. The agent that has your home and personal auto is not usually knowledgeable in the best insurance needs for residential rentals. However, specialists in residential rentals can usually offer home and personal auto insurance. Also, the specialist might not insure ALL types of residential rentals. You want to find the best in your area or state. Insurance companies will have claims people in all parts of the state, so the specialist agent does not have to be local.

Just as not all insurance agents are the same, neither are insurance policies. There are many different types of coverages and it is best to find out all you can from a reputable and experienced agent.

You want to ALWAYS have a preferred insurance company. You want to make sure that the insurance company is admitted to do business in your state and rated an "A" by A.M. Best (an independent rating insurance company).

Make sure your landlord policy has the following:

1. Replacement cost on the building
2. Loss of rents for at least 12 months or more
3. Liability of at least $1,000,000 or more (sometimes with an umbrella policy added)
4. Building Ordinance or Law coverage for code upgrades when claims happen. (Try to get at least $50,000 or more.)
5. If you have multiple locations, try to put them all on the same policy, but make sure the liability is per location. If they combine locations, then see if they will "blanket" the building limits, giving you even higher building limits

Bottom line, talk to a specialist or an agent that understands the ins and outs of being a residential landlord.

At Insurance by Castle, we are residential landlord specialists. I am a landlord as well. We have been insuring landlords since the 1940's. As specialists, we know these types of properties and the types of coverages needed. Not all insurance policies are equal. With a specialist, you have an agent that knows the market, knows what coverages are needed and, just as important, what coverages are NOT needed. At our agency, we are this and more. At Insurance by Castle, we not only have all of this, but we have "exclusive" programs for the landlord of multiple residential locations. Our most popular program is our exclusive "7 Doors or More" ™ program. This program insures seven rental units or more all on one policy. This includes single family rentals to apartment buildings. All of this is at apartment rates (the best available in California) and gives the deepest discount with the "multiple building" discount. **PLUS**, the "blanket building" endorsement is included at NO EXTRA premium.

HERE IS WHAT TO DO NEXT:

- **DETERMINE YOUR DESIRED SIZE**
- **DETERMINE IF YOU WANT TO SELF-MANAGE OR HIRE A MANAGEMENT COMPANY**
- **START DRAFTING YOUR LANDLORD POLICY**
- **CONTACT ME TO DISCUSS YOUR SPECIFIC SITUATION AND GET ANSWERS TO YOUR BURNING QUESTIONS. EMAIL – Russ@InsuranceByCastle.com or PHONE – 800-644-6443 extension 101.**

Part 5

Maximize Your Financial Windfall

Chapter 33
Tax Benefits of Rental Properties

As it is for most small businesses, the tax advantages of items that can be written off can significantly lower your tax rate. Without these write-offs, you may very likely pay so much in taxes, that your profits are eaten up. This takes your rental property from a profitable business to a losing venture. And that's not what we want at all. The good news is that rental properties typically provide more tax benefits than almost any other type of investment.

According to an article on TurboTax Inituit.com "A landlord is allowed to deduct any reasonable expenses used in the conduct, maintenance and managing of her rental properties."

Some of these deductions include:

- Utilities
- Necessary repairs and what is required for the upkeep and maintenance of the property
- Travel expenses, both local and long distance
- Insurance premiums
- Legal and professional fees
- Cost of operating your home office for the purpose of managing your rental property
- Payments made to employees or independent contractors
- Interest and taxes paid on the property. (Keep in mind that the IRS has strict criteria for these expenses, and they are scrutinized very carefully.)
- Depreciation tax shelter

- And, other expenses for these rentals

Consult your tax advisor for more information about your area.

Rental properties are considered assets. The IRS allows for a portion of your rental property to be deducted as depreciation each year over several years. It's important to note that only the value of the structure is considered in this equation. What that means is that land is not included.

Additionally, it's good to know that as a landlord, you can deduct wages and salaries for those working for you, which can make a substantial difference. Examples include residential managers and maintenance workers. Independent contractors can also be deducted, which can include: electricians, plumbers, landscapers, roofers, handymen, etc.

For independent contractors, be sure you keep their name or business name and their tax identification number or social security number for tax purposes. Most independent contractors, once they earn over $600.00, will require a Form 1099-MISC to be filed.

Occasionally there are those who don't necessarily have a plan to become a landlord. Perhaps a job opportunity arises and you need to move, but can't sell your property. You might decide the best course of action might be to rent. It's good to know that the same rules and regulations apply to you, so take note of all we cover in this book.

NOTE: Check with your tax professional as these items in this book are meant as a reference point only, and not tax advice.

One final note, as a landlord it is your responsibility to keep your personal information and that of your tenant secure. In all you do, make sure you are mindful of that. And as with everything else, if something were to happen, act promptly.

HERE IS WHAT TO DO NEXT:

- **FIND A GOOD TAX ATTORNEY TO ADD TO YOUR TEAM OF EXPERTS**
- **FAMILARIZE YOURSELF WITH ALLOWABLE DEDUCTIONS**
- **CONTACT ME TO DISCUSS YOUR SPECIFIC SITUATION AND GET ANSWERS TO YOUR BURNING QUESTIONS. EMAIL – Russ@InsuranceByCastle.com or PHONE – 800-644-6443 extension 101.**

Chapter 34
1031 Exchange & Capital Gains

When you sell an investment property you normally end up paying capital gains tax, which can be substantial. Because of this, many landlords hang on to unprofitable properties, but you don't have to. You should look into what is commonly referred to as a 1031 Exchange. A 1031 Exchange is defined under section 1031 of the IRS Code. It basically states that when your property is sold, the 1031 Exchange allows you to not pay capital gains tax as long as the property you purchase is similar and you use the monies you gained in that original sale to pay for the new property. The new loan amount must be the same or higher on the replacement property. Also of note is that it does not apply to personal property. You can't use this to move into another home.

1031 Exchange is also sometimes referred to as a "Like Kind Exchange" or "Starker Exchange."

Additional things to know include:

- An example of when it can be used would be if the property you are investing in doesn't produce the desired income and is creating more work than it's worth. You can sell that property and invest in another that might make more sense. You do this without having a significant capital gains tax. Your bad investment can then turn into a profitable venture, which, of course, is good news all around.
- Another scenario might be that you want investments in different locations for a number of

reasons. You can sell a property in one location and invest in a property at another location. This is especially beneficial today when there are numerous great opportunities in different communities. You can easily snatch up those opportunities because you've sold elsewhere.

- The property you purchased has increased substantially in value. This is a great thing except when it comes to selling and paying capital gains tax. The 1031 Exchange can help you substantially there because you now can invest those profits in a similar high-value property and not lose money paying taxes. We call that another one of our win/wins.
- You can exchange almost any type of property as long as it's not personal property.
- You can exchange a single residential property for a commercial office building. So, if you want to move into investing in commercial properties over residential properties, this will help you make that happen. Nice...right?
- And, it doesn't have to be a one-on-one exchange. You can exchange one property for multiple replacement properties.

The following properties are eligible for 1031 considerations: Businesses, Farms, Gas Stations, Golf Courses, Hotels and Motels, Apartments, Condos, Shopping Malls, Rental Properties, etc.

There are Several Types of 1031 Exchanges. They include:

Delayed Exchange – Perhaps the most common. The investor can sell their property first and, within a certain amount of time, find a replacement.

Reverse Exchange – This allows you to buy your property first and then, at a later date, pay for it. This is usually an "all cash" exchange. You can't be named on both properties (the one you are selling and the replacement one). Should be noted that some banks are hesitant to lend to you under this plan.

Construction-Improvement Exchange – This allows you to use any funds from the sale of the original property (if, for example, the replacement is less) towards construction or improvement on your new property.

As stated many times in this book, consult your legal and financial advisers for the best advice for your particular circumstances.

HERE IS WHAT TO DO NEXT:
- **FAMILARIZE YOURSELF WITH THE DIFFERENT 1031 RULES**
- **CONSULT YOUR LEGAL AND FINANCIAL ADVISORS FOR ADVICE**
- **CONTACT ME TO DISCUSS YOUR SPECIFIC SITUATION AND GET ANSWERS TO YOUR BURNING QUESTIONS. EMAIL – Russ@InsuranceByCastle.com or PHONE – 800-644-6443 extension 101.**

Chapter 35
Real Estate Investing & Inheritance

Being a landlord brings with it many responsibilities, but perhaps one that is often overlooked is the responsibility to talk to your legal and financial advisors about your inheritance. As a landlord, you work too hard not to pass the inheritance on to your family or heirs. And you want your family or heirs to pay the least amount in taxes.

First off, it is imperative to explain your plan with your family or heirs while you can. Have an open discussion. This way, there are no surprises and all parties understand your wishes well in advance.

What often happens after the death of a loved one if you haven't fully discussed it with your family or heirs, in many cases, these individuals may not be prepared for the obligations that might be presented in inheriting property. It can then go from a blessing, which is what you hope for, to a nightmare, which obviously you don't want.

It is good to talk to your tax advisor to get advice on the taxes that your family or heirs will be responsible today. In some cases, it is advisable for the owner to purchase life insurance for the sole purpose of paying the taxes so the family or heirs are not left with this expense.

I have a client that actually had to sell some rental property just to pay the taxes. As you can imagine, the timing of the sales did not allow the family to sell at the highest price available. They had to get the sale done within a window of time to pay the taxes before any penalties were charged. You don't want that to happen to you.

I had another client that was very hard working and owned over 30 rental properties. His plan was to share all these properties among his four children and ALL of his grandchildren. He worked with his financial advisor and came up with his plan. He decided to divide the properties into five even portions. The first four were for each of his children. The last piece was to be given to ALL his grandchildren when they turned 25. He had a meeting with all his children and explained how this was to work. At the time of his death, his one daughter had just found out she was pregnant. Because he had discussed his plan, all of the children knew that this grandchild, that had not been born yet, was to be part of the grandchildren's portion. It is VERY important to discuss your estate plan with your family or heirs prior to your death. This way, all people concerned can ask any questions and they can hear it from you as to your plan. If you wait until they read it in your will, there could be some confusion on certain points. If you do this in person, then all parties are present and they can ask questions.

Let's break it down further and discuss the various inheritance rules and topics.

Property Insurance - It should be noted that you can't keep the decedent's property insurance policy following his/her death once you inherit property. Once you inherit the property, you need to start a new policy under the name or entity under which you take title.

There are many options available in how the rental property can be titled: Your name - Your trust – LLC – Partnership – Corporation, etc.

Mortgage Transfer – Upon the decedent's death, you can keep the mortgage intact. A clause can be added in the mortgage papers stating that payment will become due immediately to the lender. To transfer ownership, there is what is known as a 'due-on-sale' clause and that outlines the procedure that takes place. This clause also notes that the entirety of the mortgage becomes immediately due to the lender.

Reverse Mortgage – A reverse mortgage is available to those 62 and older. The money has to be repaid to the lender and you have 30 days after the decedent's death to notify them how the payment will be done. It must be repaid, with interest, and it must be repaid fully before the real estate is theirs. You can refinance if the bank allows.

Rental - If real estate is a home loan, you might be able to rent the property without refinancing, thus allowing you to create income from the inheritance instead of selling or occupying the property. You can do this for up to three years in most areas. It's just important to familiarize yourself with all the permits, rules, etc., that apply. Seek legal counsel to be sure.

Joint Tenancy – This allows you to immediately inherit real estate upon the death of the owner. The ownership transfers without the need for a court order or even a deed change. The surviving co-owner automatically receives full ownership at the time of death without the need to file a probate petition.

Now let's talk more about other items. It's important in an inheritance to understand the different taxes that might apply.

Estate Tax: Before you cash in on your inheritance, be prepared to pay taxes. These differ from state to state, so it's important to learn what you owe for your property and your state.

Capital Gains Tax – Capital gains is a tax that is assessed on a long-term asset and is realized from the date of purchase to the date of sale. It's very important to check this out and familiarize yourself with all aspects of it. We have gone into great detail on capital gains taxes in other chapters so review those in detail.

Probate – If someone dies without a will, the inheritance can only be transferred through a court proceeding, commonly referred to as probate. This can be a lengthy, costly, and upsetting process done at a time when most are grieving. It is so important to have a will in place so that your family doesn't have to go through these proceedings.

Heirs at Law – Let's say you die without a will. Your spouse's children from a prior marriage can now be part of your Estate. **The** spouse will receive the first $50,000 and, then, will need to split the remaining estate assets with the decedent's surviving children. Check with your legal counsel to see what is applicable for you and your property.

Bottom line, consult with both your legal and financial advisors to get the best plan of action for you. I have had the meetings with both parties in the same room. This way we can talk through each scenario from both perspectives. In my case, there were issues from the legal perspective on some issues and there were tax implications on other issues. We talked through all of them and in the end, choose the best option for me, the landlord.

HERE IS WHAT TO DO NEXT:

- **ADD A FINANCIAL ADVISOR TO YOUR TEAM OF EXPERTS**
- **FAMILARIZE YOURSELF WITH THE VARIOUS INHERITANCE RULES AND TOPICS**
- **CONTACT ME TO DISCUSS YOUR SPECIFIC SITUATION AND GET ANSWERS TO YOUR BURNING QUESTIONS. EMAIL – Russ@InsuranceByCastle.com or PHONE – 800-644-6443 extension 101.**

Chapter 36
Insider Investment Tips

Life insurance in an estate plan is essential and most estate plans have this covered and have some sort of policy. It serves to pay taxes, funeral expenses, rental property expenses, debts, and more. Also, it provides money for the families or heirs you leave behind so they can best survive after you are no longer providing for them. Often times families use life insurance for education, paying off mortgages, and other expenses.

The size of the estate should also be considered. You need to ensure that it adequately takes care of not only your family, but if you are passing on the business (rentals), all that encompasses as well.

It does pay to provide for the expenses in advance. You can plan for this is a number of ways:

- Have the money in the bank, CD, or other source
- You can have Life Insurance in place to pay these expenses
- You might have to sell a property to pay the expenses on other locations (probably the choice of last resort)

Bottom line...it is a good idea to plan ahead and plan accordingly.

So, let's dive into the basics.

First of all, life insurance received by beneficiaries is generally tax-free. You can imagine what a blessing that is to those that receive it as well.

According to Investopedia.com, there are three circumstances that cause life insurance to be included in the decedent's estate:

1. The proceeds are paid to the executor of the decedent's estate.
2. The decedent at death possessed an <u>incident of ownership</u> in the policy.
3. There is a transfer of ownership within three years of death (<u>three-year rule</u> must be observed).

There are many types of life insurance. The most common these days for estate planning are either a term policy or a whole life policy.

The term policy is very simply a life insurance policy for a certain amount and the premium stays the same for a set number of years. So, a 20-year term policy would have the same premium for the first 20 years. It would still be in force beyond that term, but the premium would rise in year 21 and thereafter. Most families buy this early on to provide for the family to pay for college for the children or pay off the mortgage for the surviving parent (relieving that financial burden).

The whole life insurance policy is a "term policy" plus a "savings account." When paying the premiums, you are paying for the death benefit, plus an added portion of the premium starts to accumulate in a "savings account." This "savings account" I refer to is the cash value of the policy. This cash value is available to be borrowed against during the life of the policy or paid TAX FREE in addition to the death benefit at the time of the passing of the client.

There are many variations of this whole life policy and many endorsements that modify the policy. But these are the primary two types of life insurance used for estate planning.

In addition, there are different ways to write these policies. Some of the options are with life insurance trust arrangements. They are:

Revocable Life Insurance Trust – The trust is named as the beneficiary of life insurance policies and the grantor will retain the right to revoke the trust or revoke other rights of ownership as well. You can modify the trust if you need with a trust amendment. So, it's revocable as opposed to irrevocable.

Irrevocable – An irrevocable trust can't be changed after it has been signed. There are benefits to having this type of trust, but as always know the pros and cons of which trust would work for your situation.

Individuals should consult an experienced financial planner to determine their needs for life insurance and the types of policies that are suitable for their estate planning needs.

HERE IS WHAT TO DO NEXT:

- **DISCUSS YOUR ESTATE GOALS WITH YOUR FINANCIAL ADVISOR**
- **CONSIDER DRAFTING A WILL OR A FAMILY TRUST**
- **CONSIDER LIFE INSURANCE AS A TOOL TO PROTECT YOUR HEIRS**
- **DISCUSS USING LIFE INSURANCE AS A TOOL WITH YOUR INSURANCE AGENT**
- **REVIEW BENEFICARIES ANNUALY**
- **CONTACT ME TO DISCUSS YOUR SPECIFIC SITUATION AND GET ANSWERS TO YOUR BURNING QUESTIONS. EMAIL – Russ@InsuranceByCastle.com or PHONE – 800-644-6443 extension 101.**

Conclusion

I hope you have enjoyed this book. The purpose is to help the residential landlord. In my many years of experience as a landlord and a leading independent insurance agent for residential landlords, I have learned many things that you must know. Because I come from both sides of the situation (as a landlord and as an insurance authority), I have a unique view of these circumstances.

This book has been layed out in a way so you can read a chapter that you want to learn more about OR read the book from cover to cover.

I intentionally did not make these topics too long and wordy. I am the type of person who wants to get to the point. I hope you appreciate this approach.

Being a third-generation insurance agent, I have learned a lot of this information from my father and, then, some more from my grandfather. There are decades of first-hand knowledge in this book. Plus, I have learned from the countless clients that I have protected over many years. So, this book is first-hand practical knowledge.

You can always reach out to me through our websites at www.InsuranceByCastle.com; www.7DoorsOrMore.com; www.LandlordInsurance.com; or landing page for this book. We are also on the following social media platforms:

Facebook -
https://www.facebook.com/InsurancebyCastle/

LinkedIn - https://www.linkedin.com/in/russellcastle/

Blog - http://landlordinsuranceca.com/blog/

Plus, you can call my office at 800-644-6443. My extension is 101.

Or Email Me at Russ@InsuranceByCastle.com

I look forward to helping you in this process in any way I can!